Geraldina & the Compass Rose

One Woman's Faith-Filled
Journey to Find Love

A MEMOIR

Geraldina & the Compass Rose

One Woman's Faith-Filled
Journey to Find Love

A MEMOIR

GERALDINE BROWN GIOMBLANCO

Geraldina & the Compass Rose: A Memoir
Copyright 2019 by Geraldine Brown Giomblanco

The author has recreated events, locales, and conversations
from her memories of them. While conversations in this
book are not word-for-word transcriptions, in all instances,
the essence of the dialogue is accurate. In some instances, the
author has changed the names of individuals to maintain their
privacy.

Cover Design by Melissa Williams Design
"Searching for Peace" front cover photo ©2019 vwpix,
Adobe Stock; Yacht silhouette ©2019 Don, Adobe Stock

Interior Formatting by Melissa Williams Design

Author Photo by Patrick Colquhoun www.pc-foto.com

Edited by Kimberly Caldwell Steffen

ISBN: 978-1-7337422-0-7
(paperback edition)

Published by GBG Books

www.gbgbooks.com

I believe in love.

Saint Thérèse of Lisieux,
the Little Flower

Contents

Introduction

I have a story to tell you.

It's the tale of finding love at fifty after a thirty-year wait. And not just love, but a heart-to-heart connection with the man of my dreams. It's the tale of my Italian grandma, Rosaria, who believed in the love of God and the power of prayer. I feel her spirit inside me, guiding me now as she did in life.

It's a tale about divine providence, a guardian angel, saints, and signs from Heaven—the bountiful, improbable, goose-bump–raising signs that appeared in my life when I was on the right path to love. (And, as you will see in the pages that follow, my way to the altar was deluged with loving signs!)

First, though, I want to share the secret. It's simple, it's freely available, and you can use it, too. It is this:

You must hang on to hope.

Hope keeps you open to whatever God puts in your life. Hope allows you to see possibilities when outcomes are different from what you expect. Everyone struggles and stumbles. Everyone carries burdens, and I have my share. But even when my trust in the wrong men led me to make decisions that haunted me, I did not give up hope that my prayers would be answered.

My hope springs from knowing with every fiber of

my being that I am loved by God. And I know now that God's love is unconditional. It is as pure and constant as the innocent love of a child. I am Catholic. But I believe that any faith tradition can anchor you in the knowledge of our Creator's love. The love is there. We each can choose to wrap ourselves in its warmth.

Whenever I've faced a challenge at work or in my personal life, I pray, "God, give me guts," and then I follow my instincts as my mother taught me to do. That practice has brought career success, and it helped me dig deep inside myself for what I truly wished for in a marriage.

A list of "Fifty Things I Want in a Man" came out of that soul search, which was really about me and the things I value most in life. First and foremost, I believe in love, that state of grace that makes you want to be your best and give your best to others. I wanted that kind of love in a marital relationship.

With my list of fifty things, I set my intentions, and I prayed. I knew that I could be patient because I'd realized looking back that my decisions had always been made around finding that true soul companionship. For me, that connection is what makes the sacrament of marriage the holiest of holy things.

I want this book to encourage you to set clear intentions for what you want in your life and to find the courage to hope. I want you to feel the joy I felt when I saw the signs that led me to my husband. I also want you to know, as I do now, that nothing you've done makes you unworthy of God's love. And that fully accepting yourself—and loving yourself—is incredibly freeing.

I wrote this book to inspire you on your journey in life, because I am living proof that extraordinary things can happen to ordinary people. And dreams do come true.

Chapter One

The Man in the Airport

He was one of the most important people I would ever meet in my life, but I can't remember his face. There are so many things I can recall perfectly about him: The sound of his voice. The way he traced circles with his finger on the airport bar tabletop as he spoke. How safe he made me feel, even though I'd only met him that day. But all these years later, his face is a blur . . . and maybe that's how it's meant to be.

It was June 1995, and I was in yet another airport for yet another work trip that seemed like a waste of money and time. Why fly all the way from New York to Minnesota and back again for one holiday-planning meeting? We could have said everything that needed to be said over the phone. I was even supposed to spend the night in the North Star State, but I skipped checking in to the hotel and went straight back to Minneapolis-Saint Paul International Airport after the meeting. A night of room service in an all-expenses-paid hotel suite should have been more appealing than the thought of getting back on another plane. But as a marketing director for a company that owned and managed shopping malls across the United States, I was used to traveling for my job. Most of the time, I didn't mind. At least all the hours spent in the air (and browsing airport bookstores) meant I was able to get a lot of reading done. I was good at traveling, just like I was good at my job. Still, there were days when I'd had enough of both . . . and this was starting to feel like one of them. All the mini-bar treats in the world couldn't make up for the comfort of sleeping in my own bed.

Adding to my annoyance over having to make the trip in the first place was the fact that our flight was delayed. At the sound of the announcement crackling over the airport speakers, I could hear the exasperated travelers around me start to groan. But what was the point of complaining about something that was completely out of my control?

Determined to make the best of the situation, I headed to the restroom and swapped my work clothes for my most comfortable Eileen Fisher sweat suit. With that, I was ready to find the perfect reading material and a snack and settle in for the duration.

Scanning the shelves at the kiosk, I found myself drawn to a book with a bright-yellow cover: *Gig: Americans Talk About Their Jobs.* Instinctively, I reached for it, not knowing at the time that so many of the stories in the book would echo the professional frustrations that were brewing inside of me.

In fact, I wasn't even fully aware of how frustrated I was yet. My life looked amazing on paper. I was a healthy, successful professional rapidly ascending the ladder at a major retail real estate company, a job that took me all over the country. At thirty, I was the company's youngest regional vice president. Many people on the outside would have considered my career glamorous. I knew my friends and family thought as much, even though they knew how hard I worked. I was lucky to have people in my life who believed in me and supported me, too; just another thing about my life that seemed perfect. Still, the people closest to me also knew that my life wasn't perfect. They knew that something was missing.

At the airport, bright-yellow book in hand, I surveyed my surroundings and looked for a place to relax. Out of all the other stranded travelers, one stood out (even though, as I said, I can't remember his face). We made eye contact across the busy terminal, just like in the song "Some Enchanted Evening" from *South Pacific*: *You will see a stranger . . . across a crowded room.* Except this wasn't an enchanted evening, and the stranger I saw wasn't my Prince Charming. He turned out to be my guardian angel.

I should have been nervous when he approached me. What could this strange man who looked to be about twice my age possibly have to say? But I wasn't nervous. It was almost a feeling of recognition I had when I saw him, the way something just kind of clicks in your head when you register a face as familiar. And yet, I had no idea why he was familiar. He wasn't a celebrity; at least I didn't think so. I was sure I'd never met this man in person. So why did I feel perfectly at ease when he offered to buy me a beer? (Especially when the truth is, I didn't even like beer?)

He told me his name was Joe George. Joe George

from Atlanta, Georgia. It sounded almost like a made-up name, I thought, or a name from a children's book. He didn't tell me much else about himself that I can remember. He did mention his mother, though, saying that she had a special talent for knowing how to receive a gift. At the time, I had the feeling he was suggesting that I might be similar, and his statement would stay in the back of my mind for years. Beyond that, I learned nothing about him. I don't know if he was married or single. That wouldn't have mattered, though, because Joe George was a perfect gentleman. Never once did I think he was trying to make a move.

Joe George didn't seem to have any kind of personal agenda at all: he clearly wasn't motivated by any selfish concerns. Instead of talking about himself—something most men seemed to love to do—Joe wanted to talk about me. Except, oddly, he seemed to know a lot about my life already. Somehow, he knew I had a close relationship with my parents. He knew that I had an uncle who played an influential role in my life (my uncle Lou). But he knew other things, too; personal details that were harder to define. He told me that I had an "incredible ability to love," for one thing, and to "never lose the little girl" inside of me.

Never lose the little girl inside. How did he know? Lately, I'd been feeling more like a kid than I had since my actual childhood, for some reason—especially when I was doing something physical and freeing, like rollerblading or riding my bicycle. Sometimes, when I was biking around the park, I'd even let go of the handlebars and cruise downhill, the wind in my hair and the enthusiastic cheers of curious (usually male) on-lookers in my ears. As this image played in my mind, Joe George leaned toward me across the table.

"Never lose that feeling of excitement," he said, almost as if he were watching the scene unfold in my imagination. "You'll look back at this time ten years from now and cherish these memories. You'll need these days to remember."

I didn't fully understand what he meant at the time. Really, I didn't understand at all. But something inside was telling me that what he was saying was true.

"The year 1996 will be a significant one for you," Joe continued, still holding my gaze. His voice was quiet, and he traced the shape of a circle on the table, over and over again. My thoughts went in circles too as I followed his finger with my gaze: Who was this man? Why was this happening? Was this some kind of sign? Or was I going nuts?

"In 1996, you'll face your destiny," he said, leaning forward again. "It might be a little scary, at first." He smiled. "But it'll be okay."

I sat and stared at Joe, feeling oddly calm and completely safe at this little table in the middle of a crowded, chaotic airport. For months, I'd been feeling a sense that my life was leading up to a crucial point—that a big decision or possible turning point was on the horizon, not too far away. The very next year was 1996. Everything Joe George said only served to validate what my intuition had been hinting at for so long . . . especially what he said next.

"I feel your grandmother's presence very strongly

around you," said Joe.

"I've been feeling her around me lately, too," I said, nodding, and it was true. My grandmother and I had had an extremely special connection when she was alive, one that stayed strong even after she passed away in 1993. That's just the way she was.

Born Rosaria Gentile, she was a typical Italian matriarch—the heart of the family—and she took care of everybody, all the time. She wasn't the type to let something like death stop her from playing a role in her granddaughter's life. Of course, losing her, even at the ripe old age of eighty-six, had been an incredible blow, but I never felt like her spirit was very far away. And here was Joe George offering confirmation.

"Listen to your grandmother," said Joe. "She's been trying to tell you something, but you're not hearing her. Not yet."

I tried to tune out the noise of the airport. If I could make the world around me go silent, maybe my grandma Rosaria's voice would be clearer.

What could she be trying to tell me? That there was someone special out there for me? That I would be alone forever but happy with my life? I wondered if the message had to do with my job and whether I was on the right track. Grandma Rosaria took a while to find her own calling, after all. An Italian immigrant, her first dream was to become a nun. She even entered the convent of the School Sisters of Notre Dame, where she worked with orphaned boys. But while the other sisters would later remember her as a kind and devout person, my grandmother eventually decided that she didn't belong with them. Whether it was because the order wanted her to become a teacher when she hoped to be a seamstress or because she realized that her true vocation was to be a wife and mother, I'm not sure.

I do know that she was the most loving and devoted grandmother any kid could ever hope to have, and I never doubted her love for me—even beyond the grave. If Grandma Rosaria had something to tell me, I wanted to hear it.

Joe George and I spoke for over six hours that day in the airport. It was a chance encounter that would have been missed entirely if I had stayed in Minnesota that night as planned or had allowed myself to be so distracted by impatience and frustration over the delayed flight that I closed myself off to the opportunity. And while I could have written our meeting off as a pleasant distraction and nothing more, I knew it wasn't. I knew in my heart that it was the beginning of a new road for me, and I was certain that there were guiding forces watching over me. As he and I parted ways, I knew that he was not your average Joe, as the saying goes: he was one of those guides. But I still had so many questions.

As my plane finally took off and I prepared myself to go back to my life in New York, I thought about the noise of the airport and how I never managed to tune it out all the way. I spent so much time in airports. With all the noise in my life, would I ever be able to hear the message Heaven had for me? I raised the plastic shade and looked out the window at the endless sky, pondering what Joe George had said. He'd told me to hold on to the little girl inside me. He'd said that I would receive a gift, and that my grandmother had a message for me that I would know when I heard it. "I'm listening, Grandma," I whispered to the clouds.

It was one thirty in the morning when I finally got home, but the meeting with Joe George had affected me so profoundly that I immediately sat down to write about it in my journal. *Guess who I met today?* I wrote. *I met my guardian angel. And guess who sent him?*

Rosaria Gentile.

Chapter Two

All Saints' Day

My grandmother would say she didn't have any favorites among her grandchildren, but she would also call me her favorite when nobody else was around. I think that all her grandkids were her "favorites" in their own way, but there's no denying that my grandma Rosaria and I had a very deep bond. My mom would share this story with me: "If your grandmother found money on the floor, she would pick it up and hand it to me, saying, 'Put it away for my Geraldina!'"

I thought I was named after my grandfather Gennaro (Gerry), but my mother told me differently. I was named after Saint Gerard Majella, the patron saint of expectant mothers and unborn children. He lived from 1726 to 1755 in Italy.

My grandfather died before I was born, but Grandma Rosaria wasn't the typical Italian widow, dressed head-to-toe in black with a dour face to match. Funny and warm, my grandmother was very Americanized, and she was clever. While everyone loved my grandfather's warm, sociable personality, my grandmother was the shrewder of the two. She was the one who would quietly stash away money for years so that when a big expense came along, like a car or even a house, she could surprise her husband by suddenly producing the funds: "Here's the money we need!"

That's not to say Grandma Rosaria wasn't still an old-fashioned matriarch in some ways. When my female cousins and I started dating, she would always wave a finger at us and tell us to "wait for the three steps" (meaning the three steps to the altar) before we went too far with a boy. Her first question about any prospective suitor was always "Is he Italian?" And if a guy turned out to be no good, she would tell us to "give him the gate"—another way of saying, "Get rid of him." (My cousins and I use that expression to this day.)

At the center of everything my grandmother did was her love for her faith and her family. Grandma was always praying the rosary, and when I was there, we did it together. We'd be making meatballs and praying the rosary. We'd be chopping garlic for the sauce and praying the rosary. At the end of the day, I'd be rubbing her feet and praying the rosary. When I thought we were done, she'd say, "My sister Lena! Let's pray for her." My mother cut her off when she started to pray for soap opera characters, saying, "Ma, they're not even real people!"

Grandma Rosaria was probably the most influential person in my life, especially because we lived with her until I was nine years old. She and my uncle Lou lived on the first floor of a two-family home in Yonkers, New York, and my parents, both in their early twenties, lived on the second floor with two babies, my older brother and me. Grandma loved my father and treated him like a son because she knew he was genuinely a good man and deeply in love with her daughter. I grew up expecting to marry a man whom my parents would feel that way about.

A grandmother's love is different than a mother's, and it may even be stronger sometimes, depending on the other demands in the mother's life. My grandmother recognized something in me, something that seemed to set me apart. Right from the start, special things happened for me—like when my teachers pulled me from a crowd of my peers to do special things like place a wreath of flowers on the head of the statue of the Blessed Virgin Mary during the May crowning procession at Saint Barnabas Catholic School or to lay a wreath on the tomb of the unknown soldier at Arlington National Cemetery as part of an American Legion ceremony. Whatever it was about me that made those things happen was something my grandmother cherished and encouraged.

On the day of my first Holy Communion, for which I wore a white dress, white shoes, a little white purse, and my mother's wedding veil trimmed to fit me, I was walking on air. I was absolutely joy filled. Not just because it also happened to be my seventh birthday and my parents had given me a pink ballet tutu; and not just because my aunts, uncles, and cousins from both sides of the family were there, and my aunt Vera had given me a birthstone ring—an aquamarine set in a silver band—that made me feel like a grown-up. There was something else so expansive inside me that I felt the sensation for days afterward.

For years, I considered that day to have been the best of my life. That pure elation, I now know, was the feeling of being one with God and walking the path He had set for me. It's what Grandma Rosaria had. It's what shone in her eyes no matter what she was doing. But it wasn't until decades later when I felt it again that I truly understood.

* * *

As a little girl, I loved giving gifts—to my friends, to my family, to anyone I could—even if they were my own possessions. This drove my mother nuts at times, but my grandmother understood.

"Stop giving your things away!" my mother scolded me one day in the kitchen. "We bought that Barbie doll for you, not for your friend down the street! She has her own parents to buy things for her!"

But they hadn't bought one for her, and the look of joy on her face when I gave her mine was more than worth it. "I thought it was a good thing to give to others," I said.

"*Aspetta*," my grandmother said to my mother. "Hold on. It's better to give than to receive. You have a child who's a giver. What do you want? A child who takes?"

My mother knew it, of course. "I should have named you Rosie, after your grandmother," she said to me.

Through her constant prayer and acts of everyday generosity (always with a string of rosary beads in her hand), Grandma Rosaria taught me that it's truly through giving that we receive. If unexpected visitors dropped by (and it was normal in those days for people to show up unannounced), it didn't matter how tired my grandmother was—she would be standing at the stove with her apron on. She'd whip out the pastina and "beat the daylights" out of an egg, adding plenty of Parmesan and butter (and maybe even the sign of the cross) until it was the perfect consistency. It was a recipe to soothe the soul, she said, and it always worked.

These acts of service brought her peace and joy because she offered everything she did up to God to show her love for Him. That's why going to church meant so much to her—because she loved receiving His spirit and becoming more like Him. Everything was love. This approach to life made such an impression on me that I have carried it with me through my adulthood. Work was never just about money for me; if someone needed my help, I stayed late. If a client needed extra support on the weekend, I would be there. And, like my grandmother, I was always, always praying to my angels and saints as I worked. It wasn't something I did in a conscious way or even thought about for a long time; talking to Heaven was just something I did. I even prayed to the spirits of family members who had passed away. Like my grandmother, I truly believed that they were watching over me.

My mother, on the other hand, didn't like thinking about spirits. She could hardly bring herself to attend funerals—perhaps because her own father had died when she was just eighteen. But the darkness didn't scare me because my grandmother had turned the light on in my heart and soul. She was the foundation of my faith.

Grandma Rosaria was everything to me, so I was absolutely devastated when we had to move, even though I was happy about the reason: my baby brother, Richie, was on the way. Our new home was thirty-three miles away, in Somers, New York. That might not sound very far away, but back in the 1970s, I felt like we'd moved to another country. (Or as everyone in Yonkers would say, "You're moving to the boonies!")

My parents did their best to get me excited about the new house, which my father built on a piece of land that his parents had split between his siblings and him. My brothers and I helped him, and we had pizza parties in the house as it went up. Grandma Brown gave me a picture-perfect little girl's bedroom: a pink-gingham canopy bed, white French provincial furniture with the gold wash that was popular at the time. I had a tall bureau and a wide one with a mirror over it, and Grandma Brown knitted a set of pink pillows to match the gingham. While my other grandmother kept a simple home, Grandma Brown was like Martha Stewart. Her father, my Great-grandpa Sokoloff, was a Russian cathedral painter and no doubt the source of her creativity. Her home was beautiful, with everything always in its place, and she made it look effortless.

Grandma Brown wasn't as warm and fuzzy as my Italian grandmother was. She was a TV sports fanatic and watched all her favorite New York teams religiously, a cigarette hanging out of her mouth. (So she wasn't *exactly* like Martha Stewart!) She was short and round and adorable. If you looked up the word *grandmother* in the dictionary, her picture would be there, except for the cigarette, of course. Grandma Brown was a straight shooter, so when she told my mother I was "one in a million," she meant it.

I was thrilled with my new life—especially with sledding down to Dean's Pond, which froze so deeply that my dad could drive a plow onto it to clear our skating area—but I missed Grandma Rosaria terribly. I hung the rosary beads she gave me from the bedpost so that I could hold them in my hand as I went to sleep at night, passing each bead through my fingers and sending every Hail Mary up to the Blessed Mother for my grandmother's soul. I was only nine years old, but already I knew that someday she would be gone. Lying under the canopy in the dark, I could feel that loss as if it already happened. Sometimes I would fall asleep crying.

I lived for our trips back to Yonkers to visit Grandma Rosaria. I remember running down the walk to her wooden front door with the little diamond-shaped window at the top. It was too high for me to see through when we got to the door, but from a distance I could see my grandmother's sweet little face peeking out. She was always so excited to see us. It broke my heart that her heart was broken. It made me so happy to see her again, to walk around the yard with her and listen as she told me all about the beautiful flowers that she'd planted around her statue of the Virgin Mary. My favorites were the forget-me-nots and the tea roses, as she called them.

Roses were a very meaningful flower to my grandmother for several reasons. Obviously, her name—Rosaria—was one of them. Another was her ongoing devotion to Saint Thérèse of Lisieux, or "the Little Flower." A Carmelite nun who died of tuberculosis at the age of twenty-four, Saint Thérèse loved roses. Before she died, she promised that she would spend her time in Heaven doing good on earth, and that she would "let fall a shower of roses." Those who pray to her often report roses coming to them as signs that their petitions have been answered.

My grandmother even named my mother Teresa, after the Little Flower, whose image is on a medal her father carried in his pocket. The Little Flower was especially popular at that time, thanks to stories about her sending roses to soldiers in World War I.

My grandmother's fascination with the saints, especially Saint Thérèse, fascinated me in turn. So, I was always watching for signs that she might be watching over me or sending me a message, particularly during significant or challenging times. But it wasn't until much later in my life that I began to pray my intentions to Saint Thérèse.

My mother had given me a statue that I assumed was the Virgin Mary. I kept it on my nightstand. One day, she called and asked if I still had the Saint Thérèse statue, and I said no. But when she visited me later, she saw it in my bedroom. "This is Saint Thérèse, not the Blessed Mother," she said. It was almost as if Saint Thérèse was making herself known to me slowly as I became aware of what she stood for in the Catholic faith. And after that, the more I looked for signs that she heard my prayers, the more I saw. Roses would become one of the defining themes of my life.

Another saint I felt connected to had a coincidentally similar name: Mother Teresa. I felt that way even before the famed nun and missionary technically became a saint. My grandmother admired Mother Teresa while she was still alive and passed that appreciation on to me. Her selflessness and tenacity inspired me. In 1998, I was living in Long Beach, New York, and feeling upset by the number of homeless people (particularly young people) in town. It was a problem I didn't expect to see in a community like Long Beach, and I felt compelled to help, so I signed up to be a mentor to troubled youth.

I wanted to do whatever I could, but I still felt a sense of unrest about the situation. Why was I so fortunate when these kids were struggling? Why had I been blessed with so much when others had so little? I worried that I didn't have anything to offer them, or that my help would be meaningless.

I was even having trouble sleeping. One night, as I tossed and turned at 2:00 a.m., I flipped on the TV in my bedroom, hoping for some much-needed distraction. On the screen was a famous blonde anchorwoman, speaking with none other than Mother Teresa. Why the network decided to replay an interview with Mother Teresa from earlier that year at two o'clock in the morning, I had no idea, but it was exactly what I needed to see at that moment.

"Mother Teresa, how do you do what you do?" the

journalist asked on the screen.

"There are those who can, and those who can't," Mother Teresa answered. "I can."

I turned off the TV.

"Thank you, Mother Teresa," I said aloud. "I can help, and that's all I need to know."

Friends always told me, "You're like an empath. You *feel* other people." I had been that way since childhood. But something shifted in my heart and mind that night. I vowed to embrace my gift for empathy and turn it into action. The truth was that despite the differences in our circumstances, those homeless kids and I were more alike than different. And because I had been blessed with opportunity and means, it was my responsibility to help.

* * *

That night wasn't the last time I heard from Mother Teresa. Some twenty years later, in 2009, she made her voice heard even louder.

That was the year I met my dear friend Geraldine Berger. My mother was the one who put me in touch with Gerri, and the way she came to meet her is a story all on its own. One day, my mother's best friend, Marina, got a phone call out of the blue from a woman who claimed to be her niece. It turned out that Marina's late brother Julius might have fathered a daughter years ago who was put up for adoption—and Gerri Berger thought she was that daughter. Eventually, DNA testing would prove her wrong. But when my mother heard about Gerri Berger, she decided that we had to get to know each other.

"Geraldine, you have the same initials and the same first name," my mother told me over the phone. "You're both forty-four years old, and you're both left-handed. You have to meet."

I was unemployed at the time, having recently left my toxic, high-pressure job in Boston to come home to New York and start my consulting firm, Geri Brown & Company. I was temporarily coasting on my severance package and had a little extra time on my hands, so I agreed to meet up with Gerri Berger.

As usual, my mother's instincts were right on the money. Gerri Berger and I became instant best friends, and we later expanded the list of coincidences that brought us together: it turned out we had been delivered at the same hospital by the same doctor. It was he who gave Gerri the name *Geraldine*.

Gerri was raised Jewish and I was Catholic, but the important thing was that we were both spiritual. We were soul sisters. Gerri was beautiful and outgoing and brilliant, and eventually dedicated her life to helping adopted people find their birth parents. Since I was single and Gerri was divorced, we were both in the mindset of wanting to go out and mingle. We enjoyed each other's company so much that it didn't even matter if we ended up meeting any potential partners on our excursions. We made the perfect partners in crime at that time.

One night, Gerri asked me to come out with some of her friends from high school. It happened to be All

Saint's Day—November 1, 2009. When I met Gerri at the restaurant, the first thing she did was introduce me to the owner, an older gentleman named Munther Farr. Munther had a Middle Eastern look to him, with dark hair and dark skin. He shook my hand graciously, and I went to sit down with Gerri and her old pals. Before long, it became apparent that this was going to be one of those nights where I would play the odd woman out. Gerri was having a great time flirting and reminiscing, but I just wasn't in the mood to sit through a series of high school stories from people I'd never met before, especially when I wasn't interested in anybody at the table. I was honestly more interested in watching the World Series between the Phillies and the Yankees, which was playing on a TV over the bar.

I excused myself to go and get a refill, thinking I could escape the boring conversation for a few minutes and get a better view of the game. Munther came over to wait on me himself.

"Can I interest you in a nightcap?" Munther smiled. "Cognac, perhaps?"

"Sure," I said, smiling back. I'd developed a taste for good cognac over my years of business dinners.

Munther poured the cognac into the glass, and I held it up to my nose, enjoying the fragrance.

"Do you know what today is?" I asked Munther. I didn't wait for him to answer. "It's All Saint's Day."

"Is it?" Munther poured himself a cognac and sat down on the chair next to me. "I didn't know."

"I'm really excited about it, because I teach catechism to fourth graders, and I asked our monsignor to come in and talk to them about what it takes to become a saint," I said. I had no idea why I was bringing this up with a stranger in a bar at 10:00 p.m. Gunther seemed intrigued, though, so I kept talking.

"My favorite saint is Mother Teresa," I said. "Although, she's not really a saint yet. She's just blessed." The term *blessed* is sort of one step below *saint*, referring to those who have been beatified by the church (a designation requiring one attested miracle and allowing veneration by that person's local church. Canonization, by comparison, requires two attested miracles and allows veneration by the universal Church).

Munther's jaw dropped. For a second, I almost thought he was going to fall off his chair. He looked at me with tears in his eyes.

"Are you okay?" I asked.

"I have something to show you, you're not going to believe this," he said. "Can you wait right here?"

"Of course," I said.

Munther disappeared into his office and returned with a plastic sleeve full of papers. He pulled out an airplane boarding pass.

"This was Mother Teresa's boarding pass," he said, his hands shaking.

Munther explained that he'd had these documents since 1987. He kept them in his safe. Years ago, he was a catering officer for the airline where his wife at the time, Cathleen, worked as a flight attendant. Cathleen had been planning a trip to Bangkok, where she liked to shop, when the airline scheduled her instead to work a flight from John F. Kennedy International Airport in

New York to Egypt. Her initial frustration turned to gratitude when Mother Teresa boarded the plane. She was going to Egypt to open an orphanage.

When Mother Teresa got to the gate, Munther said, she wanted to sit in coach. Cathleen wouldn't hear of it and insisted she sit in first class. Again, Mother Teresa said no. They went back and forth like this until finally she consented to sit in first class on one condition: that she could take the leftover food from the flight to her new mission in Egypt. Cathleen agreed, and she contacted Munther, who collected the leftover meals from many flights that day and sent them to the new orphanage as well.

Mother Teresa wrote a thank-you note to him by hand, and Munther saved that along with her boarding pass. It read: *Be holy like Jesus, for Jesus loves you. Love others as he loves you and God bless you, Teresa.*

"She was holy, and people could feel it," Munther told me. He shook his head in wonder. "It's like my wife said, she never knew what it felt like to be in the presence of someone holy until Mother Teresa stepped on that plane."

Munther's wife donated all the money she'd been planning to spend shopping in Bangkok to Mother Teresa's mission. And not only did the leftover food on the plane leave with her, but the passengers also took up a collection among themselves for the cause.

Munther looked down at the boarding pass and note in his hands. He'd also saved her business card, on which her address is in Bethlehem.

"It's the strangest thing, Geri," he said. "I haven't

taken these things out since the eighties, and I was just looking at them this morning. These things were meant for you to take and show to the children you teach. That's what Mother Teresa wants you to do."

Just holding the papers in my hand, I felt a thrill. The monsignor was coming to my catechism class to talk about how people become saints. Mother Teresa was in the news, and I had planned a lesson about her. I imagined the ripple effect Munther's story would have. When I had children of my own, they would grow up hearing it, and they would tell their children. I was responsible for planting this seed in fertile soil, and I would start with my catechism class. But what if something happened to these priceless relics when they were in my possession?

"Munther, I can't take these," I protested. "Just make me copies. I can show those to the kids."

He wouldn't hear of it. "No, no, I want you to have the originals to show them," he said. "You can bring them back to me when you're done. I trust you."

"I'll take excellent, excellent care of these," I promised.

I couldn't wait to get back to my apartment to get a closer look at the mementos. I made my way back over to Gerri and tapped her on the shoulder to let her know I was going home. She was so focused on catching up with her old friends that she didn't mind at all.

Driving home, I could barely contain myself. I was awakening to the realization that my intuition was God's voice coming to me through his Holy Spirit. That intuition was telling me I had a message, and it seemed to be coming straight from Mother Teresa. Munther was the conduit, and I was the messenger, meant to spread Mother Teresa's spirit to my catechism class. They would carry it with them as they grew, taking it out into the world with them. I was merely tossing the pebble into the stream; the ripple effect would do the rest. As I drove, I said a little prayer in my head. "Thank you for trusting me, Mother Teresa."

But I doubted myself. I wasn't sure I should be the person to carry this message. One of the first things I did when I got home that night was google "Mother Teresa." I already knew a fair amount about her, but there were still plenty of things I didn't know; for example, while she was born in Albania, she later became a citizen of India. It had been a long night, though, and my eyes were tired.

I also started wondering what happened with the World Series. So, I opened the armoire in my room and sank down on the edge of my king-size bed with the remote in my hand. I expected the game, or at least the news about the game, to be on Fox News, like it had been at the bar, but it wasn't. I started clicking around but couldn't find it anywhere—until finally, I found it on a Spanish-language station.

As I was trying to figure out what was going on, the TV suddenly went black. The number on the clock switched to 11:11 (11:11 on November 1, 2009). The TV instantly came back on, this time tuned to the Indian channel.

I just sat in awe for a moment. A few minutes earlier, I'd been reading about Mother Teresa becoming an

Indian citizen and now, suddenly, my TV was turning to the Indian channel all by itself. Either I was going crazy, or Heaven was confirming its divine message for me. Overwhelmed and exhausted, I decided it was time for bed. But before I got under the covers something told me to look at that boarding pass one last time. I carefully pulled it out of the plastic sleeve and examined it. The date on the pass jumped out at me: November 11.

Some things are coincidence, but this was no coincidence. This incredible example of synchronicity was proof to me that grace is real. I knew in that moment that it is possible for your heart to carry a spirit into the physical world. As a child, I'd wondered why Grandma Rosaria went to mass every day. Now I knew: she went to receive God, the bread of life. She wanted him inside her. He made her a better person. Mother Teresa, Saint Thérèse, my grandmother . . . these spirits were guiding me and speaking to my soul. All I had to do was trust that inner voice and pay attention to the signs around me.

Chapter Three

Working Girl

My first big career break came after I graduated from Berkeley College in White Plains, New York, with a degree in fashion marketing and management. I'd been something of a star at Berkeley, especially in my sales class. The final assignment was to sell something to the rest of the class, and because my mother just returned from a Princess cruise (which she documented by taking tons of gorgeous photos), I decided to peddle a trip on the cruise line. I put the photos to perfect use in a slideshow set to Lionel Richie's "All Night Long," even including pics of my mother stepping way outside her comfort zone dressed as a more modest version of a Playboy bunny in a Halloween-themed nautical fashion show.

For the presentation, I took my cue from *Love Boat* cruise director Julie McCoy and greeted every student at the door with a big smile and a cordial handshake. The music played as people took their seats, and I asked everyone to fill out index cards with their names and addresses for a chance to win a "free cruise" I promised to announce at the end. I interviewed my mother in advance about the food and activities and what the cabins were like so I could accurately describe the experience as I clicked through the photos of happy travelers sunning themselves in deck chairs and beautiful ocean sunsets. I distributed handouts and full-color brochures and tried as hard as I could to get everybody excited about taking a Princess cruise.

Not only did my method work, it worked a little too well. At the end of my presentation, everybody wanted to know why I hadn't picked a raffle winner. They thought I was really giving away a free cruise!

Word got around at Berkeley about that presentation, and teachers and administrators congratulated me. Mrs. Lentz, the placement director, was one of the most important people to take notice. There was something about her that reminded me of the Bride of Frankenstein (probably the shocking streak of gray hair that stood out against her otherwise pitch-black locks), but she was a lovely woman. We got along well. She was the kind of person who recognized talent, and she was a true mentor for me. I could always count on her when I needed guidance or a connection.

As I approached graduation, I told her how much I would love to work for a magazine or be a sales rep for a clothing line. Mrs. Lentz had relationships in the garment industry, but she let me know that she wouldn't send just anybody for an interview; she only sent those who wouldn't embarrass her. "You're at the top of my list," she told me.

"Whenever you're out there making connections, you always want to be at the top of the list. People want to deal with people they like, not people they don't," she said. *"That's* how to get to the top."

Mrs. Lentz's philosophy became my own, and it served me well. She helped me land my absolute dream job: working for Condé Nast at *Mademoiselle* magazine as the assistant to the shoes and accessories editor. I was beyond excited.

I graduated in the spring, and the job wouldn't start until August, when the current assistant would have her baby. So, I had the whole summer to work my restaurant job, go to the beach, and get ready for my first big career move.

That fantasy shattered when I got a call from *Mademoiselle* telling me that they were so sorry, but the assistant's maternity leave was going to be temporary instead of permanent, so they wouldn't be needing me after all.

I was back to square one and starting to feel desperate. Living at home wasn't working anymore. My mother and I were getting under each other's skin in the ways young-adult children and their parents often chafe against the restraints of cohabitation. There was no ill will between us. Our relationship was just suffering the usual growing pains that occur when a mother is forced to witness her daughter making decisions outside of her once-powerful influence.

My mother wanted me to pay fifty dollars per month for rent—which was admittedly reasonable, but I was making very little money and trying to save up enough cash to move out. Plus, even though my mother was always annoyed at me, she didn't really want me to leave.

She didn't even want me to work in Manhattan,

where the career opportunities were, because of my two-hour commute each way.

I called Mrs. Lentz for advice, and she immediately sent me out for a new round of interviews, confident something good was on the horizon.

Things went even better than she expected. While most of the other girls in my class were still job hunting, I got offers from Evan Picone, Esprit, and Leslie Fay.

Mrs. Lentz was thrilled. "You've got your pick of the crop," she said. "Unbelievable!"

"Which one do I take?" I had no idea what to do.

"Go with the busiest one," Mrs. Lentz said. "Leslie Fay is on fire right now."

At that time, Leslie Fay owned the incredibly popular Sassoon jeans line as well as the official *Dynasty* and *Dallas* TV collections—and everybody wanted to dress like Krystle Carrington and Pam Ewing in those days!

"They're one of the hottest showrooms in Manhattan. The only thing is . . ." Mrs. Lentz paused. "You're going to start out as a receptionist."

"I'm going to be answering phones?" Secretarial work wasn't exactly what I had in mind when I got my degree.

"It's called working your way up," said Mrs. Lentz. "Everybody does it."

I had just seen the movie *Working Girl*, in which Melanie Griffith plays a secretary at a Wall Street investment bank who shoots up the corporate ladder after she connects some financial dots and gets a brilliant idea for a merger. Making connections and going against the norm were my strong suits, and I was inspired.

Mrs. Lentz knew the industry inside out. If she said Leslie Fay was the job to take, it was the job to take. So, I took it.

Every morning I stepped on a Metro North car at the Somers train station and started the first leg of my two-hour commute, filled with the kind of optimism most of the hardened businesspeople traveling alongside me had lost years ago. Once I got into the city, the real mad dash began. If my train was just a couple of minutes late (which is not an uncommon occurrence, as any commuter can tell you), I had to sprint from Grand Central Terminal to the Leslie Fay office at Thirty-Ninth Street and Broadway. If I didn't show up exactly on time, the office manager would scream obscenities at me until the veins bulged in his neck. On rainy days, I would run through buildings and hide under awnings. Anything to avoid trying to zigzag my way through the crowd with an umbrella, which was sure to get tangled up in other umbrellas or poke somebody in the eye. I was netting $176 a week, and it cost me $20 just to get up in the morning. But I was determined to work in Manhattan despite my mother's misgivings.

I was the first person whom visitors saw through the big, glass showroom doors when they got off the elevator on our floor. There was a PA system and a gigantic switchboard on the side of my desk, and it was my job to announce people, put calls through, and, in general, present a smiling face and a friendly personality to the world.

It sounds easy enough, but the job was much harder than it looked due to the volume of calls and appointments. I found out after I accepted the position that the company had been through something like thirty receptionists in the last two months. That explained why the desk was such a mess when I arrived!

Determined not to become just another number, I buckled down. I organized my desk to perfection and tried to connect with everyone who came through the showroom. It took a tremendous amount of focus to keep up with the workload, but I managed. I even started getting bold. When people refused to pick up their calls after I tried to patch them through multiple times, I was supposed to write down the messages on little pink slips and put them in their message boxes. Sometimes these calls would turn out to be important, and I'd inevitably get yelled at: "Why didn't you tell me so-and-so was on the phone?" But I refused to back down. "I'm not your personal secretary," I would say. "I tried to send you the call three times! Please have the courtesy to pick up your phone!"

Rose was the woman who trained me, and she was like an angel who appeared to guide me through the chaos of the New York City fashion world. She would cover me when I was on break (not that I got breaks very often). "Girl, they're never going to promote you," she used to say, shaking her head. "You're doing too good a job!"

Not counting my immediate supervisor—the guy with the bulging neck veins—most of the people I worked with were encouraging—and entertaining, too.

Besides Rose, there was Camille, who was Italian and called me "doll" or "babe." Terri was a heavyset Jewish woman who favored patent-leather loafers and stirrup pants and always had her nails done. (At Leslie Fay, it seemed almost everyone was either Italian or Jewish, me included.) The assistant designer, who went by the alias *Sophia*, looked like a grown-up version of Spanky from *The Little Rascals* with his black-rimmed eyeglasses. Like Terri, he was often in stirrup pants. Mike, the controller, used to pull me aside when I was having a bad day to tell me I was doing a great job.

The more support I got from my coworkers, the bolder I became. Sometimes sales reps would show up to see the buyers without an appointment. This was strictly against protocol, but if I thought a project looked promising, I'd sneak them through anyway.

What it all came down to, I guess, was the fact that I had guts—something the thirty secretaries who warmed my seat before me apparently did not have. As a newcomer in an office where relationships were long-standing and the power hierarchy was already firmly in place, being gutsy was a risk. I easily could have been seen as insubordinate and shut out of the group. Instead, most of the people in the office appreciated my suggestions, even if they resisted at first.

The acceptance of my coworkers meant a lot to me, but the person whose opinion mattered the most was my boss, Arthur Levine. As a powerful industry vet, Arthur could be difficult, for sure. He was the kind of person who'd scream and yell if I didn't get his coffee right. (Even if it was the guy at the deli downstairs who screwed up and not me!) But I could handle Arthur's hot temper because he liked me. Arthur respected initiative and hard work, and I think he got a kick out of my spunk. Whatever it was about me that Arthur liked, knowing that he believed in me gave me even more motivation to do my best.

So did fear of disappointing him, and I sometimes found myself doing things that scared me to death.

Case in point: One day, when I was eating my lunch in the back room, Rose came running in looking for me.

"Geri," she said, breathless. "The fit model didn't show up for the *Dynasty* suit fitting, and you're the perfect size. Arthur wants you to do it instead."

I nearly choked on my sandwich. "Are you crazy?" *Dynasty* stars Linda Evans and Joan Collins were hot— they were in the tabloids all the time, and the boss wanted *me* to be their fit model?

"I ran all the way from Grand Central this morning, and people have been screaming at me since I got to my desk," I said. "I'm all sweaty, and I have my ugly bra on. I'm totally unprepared!"

Rose gave me a look. "Geri, it's Arthur!"

She was right. One didn't say no to Arthur Levine. It would have been career suicide. So, I said okay. In the fitting room, I stood behind a three-paneled divider and buttoned up a silk blouse with a big, oversized bow. The style in those days was to exaggerate everything— shoulders were padded, and bows, the feminine version of the "power suit" necktie, were big and floppy. As the designers bustled around me, tugging and prodding and pinning, I prayed that the sweat dripping from my armpits wouldn't ruin the fabric. And when I say I prayed, I mean I actually made the sign of the cross.

If it hadn't been for Arthur and my coworkers pushing me out of my comfort zone, I might never have learned to become truly comfortable with myself. My job at Leslie Fay was where I started to build my self-esteem and learn to challenge myself. I didn't feel discouraged anymore when I came up against obstacles; I felt determined. Sure of myself. Like the way I managed the switchboard, after a while I was able to organize everything for maximum efficiency. The more I accomplished, the more accomplished I felt. And even though I was stressed out beyond belief on a daily basis, when it came down to it, I liked all the different angles of the business. I liked the way it felt to be able to read a room. I wasn't an office kind of girl at heart, but I liked being at the center of so much activity. I also valued being in the company of so many smart and talented people, and I was so grateful that they valued my input, too.

I felt even more valued around the holidays, when the gifts started piling up on my desk. Everyone from buyers to salespeople to clients who regularly came through the office showered me with presents: wine, perfume from Paris, silk lingerie, a phone with a built-in clock (very fancy back then), lunches out, even straight-up cash. I wasn't the new kid anymore; I was officially part of the team.

Still, I didn't want to be a receptionist forever. The more time I spent at Leslie Fay, the more I wanted to get into sales. With my outgoing personality and my ability to tune into what people wanted, I knew I could be a success. Since everything had been going so well, I thought it would be reasonable for me to ask Mike, the controller, about the likelihood of a promotion. The answer he gave me was an honest one—and complimentary, too—but it wasn't exactly what I wanted to hear.

"Geri, you're doing an amazing job," Mike said, closing the door to his office. "You run the show around here, and Arthur loves you. The problem is, they're never going to find anybody to replace you. You've set the bar too high."

Mike paused, shaking his head. "My advice to you is to get out of here. Until you find something else, learn everything you can. But start thinking about moving on."

I was incredibly lucky to have a mentor like Mike giving me the inside scoop. Someone else in his position might have fed me some kind of line about putting time in and working my way up and paying dues, but Mike was a true leader. He didn't want to hold me back, even if that meant losing me as an employee. That was a lesson in leadership I never forgot.

Chapter Four

Love Italian Style

I didn't have to go very far to find my next gig—in fact, I didn't even have to leave the building. There was only one showroom on our floor besides Leslie Fay. That company was Tower Dresses, it was looking for an assistant sales rep for its special-occasion wear. With Mike's encouragement, I applied . . . and was hired, much to my shock and delight.

There I was, a bona fide career girl at last, doing a job I trained for and actually wanted to do. I'd seen the hefty commissions my coworkers at Leslie Fay earned, and soon, I hoped, I'd be making the money I wanted to make, too. Commuting into the city every day, particularly for a job in the fashion industry, I was surrounded by glamorous people. Unfortunately, I didn't have their glamorous clothing budget. I was forced to get creative, scouring sale racks and hitting all the sample sales, which were a fantastic way to buy designer clothes on the cheap. Most of the time, I think I pulled off the young, chic professional look pretty well—even if I had to wear the same pieces every week.

I also started going to the gym regularly. Just because I didn't have a closet full of designer clothes didn't mean I couldn't have a designer body! I would park my car at the Armonk train station and work out at a gym called The Barn, adding to the exercise I already got running from Grand Central to the office and back again. It was at The Barn that I met Paige.

Paige was part Westchester housewife, part hippie chick from the 1960s. Not everybody "got" Paige—she was too "out there" for some people. But Paige and I clicked. She and her husband, Stan, lived in upscale Chappaqua, New York, but they also had an apartment on a moneyed private street in New York City. Stan was a real estate bigwig, with properties all over Riverdale and Manhattan. Some of them were in the notoriously expensive diamond district. So, Paige and Stan, as you can imagine, had quite an impressive net worth. At that point, though, I had zero awareness of things like net worth. All I knew was that I liked them both, and as it turned out, they liked my strong values . . . enough to trust me with their daughter, Rebecca.

Rebecca was four and a half years old, and Paige needed a part-time babysitter. I was working full time at the showroom but still not making the amount of money I really needed, and since my weekends were free (no boyfriend) and I loved kids, I told her I would be happy to meet Rebecca.

I'll never forget the day we met. Paige and Stan's Chappaqua home was just twenty minutes away from my parents' house in Somers. At the time, I was driving a yellow Firebird that I inherited from my aunt. It had black bucket seats and way more horsepower than I needed. (The very day I got it, I got a speeding ticket.)

When I drove up the long hill to Paige and Stan's house, Rebecca was outside tooling around on her Hot Wheels tricycle. She was beyond adorable, with milky white skin, gigantic dimples, and black hair cut Cleopatra style, the straight bangs falling over clear blue eyes.

I opened the door to get out of my car, and Rebecca came skidding to a stop on her trike. She looked me up and down. "You must be my new babysitter," she said. She had a slight lisp, and she seemed to be smirking.

"I might be," I said, smiling.

"I gotta tell you one thing," Rebecca said. Her face was serious. "You give me chocolate, I'll be bouncing off the walls."

And with that classic one-liner, I fell head over heels in love with Rebecca. We were like magic together, and that magic was contagious. I would take her to the park, and we'd end up with a trail of other kids latching on to our games, following us around. I felt like the Pied Piper. Honestly, it was a blast. And half the time, when I was babysitting Rebecca at her house, Paige and Stan didn't even leave. We all got along so well (like family, really), they'd often take me out to dinner afterward, too. Plus, they paid me twenty-five dollars an hour, which was unheard of in 1986 for a babysitting job.

I was making progress at my new job, too, landing big-time accounts for a newcomer. In some ways, my inexperience was a bonus. I attempted the impossible because I didn't know any better. One day as we prepared for fashion week, my bosses (who were Hasidic Jewish twin brothers) dropped a giant book on my desk filled with names of boutiques and department stores nationwide and told me to start making appointments for the "petite" line. That was the extent of their instructions—and the beginning of me trying to figure out things out on my own.

I didn't know which of the stores on the list were already clients and which weren't; I didn't know which were considered long shots. So, I just started calling. I called and called and called and talked and talked and talked. I was friendly and bubbly and started conversations about trends and how I got in the business and whatever else the person on the other end of the line seemed interested in. My sales style was conversational, never phony. "You have to see the line; it's just exquisite," I would say. I even mailed thank you notes after appointments, which owners of everything from urban boutiques to bridal shops in Mississippi appreciated.

Because we had so many big department stores for clients, I just assumed Nordstrom was one of them when I called and made an appointment for the retailer's buyer from the West Coast to check out our new line. When the buyer showed up, it was as if a shock of electricity went through the office. Apparently, this woman was a major deal with tremendous influence—though, of course, I had no idea who she was. "What is she doing here?" everyone whispered. The Nordstrom woman told our front-desk gal that she had an appointment with someone named "Geri"—and the receptionist seated her in the showroom of a man named Jerry!

Jerry was hilarious. He was a small, sweet guy with a dry sense of humor, and luckily, he managed to figure out that the buyer was supposed to be meeting with me, not him. When the woman was finally seated across from me in my office, she smiled.

"You know," she said, leaning forward. "No one from your company has ever just called me up and invited me here before. No one has ever showed me that level of respect."

My coworkers were hovering outside the showroom floor just in case I needed to be rescued. But I didn't need their help. I handled the Nordstrom buyer just like any other client, with courtesy and deference. I didn't brownnose. I just did my job, showing her the line and pointing out which pieces were selling better than others. I made the usual suggestions, noting where changes could be made and details could be added or taken away. I brought the designer in to discuss any necessary alterations. And, just as I'd hoped, the Nordstrom buyer placed an order.

It was a huge jewel in my crown as far as my bosses were concerned. Even though I still wasn't making commission, the twins told me they were happy with my performance and decided to promote me to the "Missy" line of special-occasion wear.

I started staying later at work and spending more time in the city in general. Thankfully, I knew a lot of people—some of them former coworkers from the Leslie Fay showroom, who often needed apartment sitters, which helped to cut down on my commute time. Staying in other people's places gave me some of my favorite New York City memories ever, like watching the Macy's Fourth of July Fireworks light up the city skyline from a gorgeous rooftop.

Paige and Stan let me use their apartment on Sutton Place, a small and exclusive street on the easternmost part of Manhattan. I would babysit Rebecca there on weekends sometimes and was always included in family celebrations, from over-the-top children's birthday parties to steak dinners at Tony Roma's. Since my career was taking off, Paige had started calling me "Geri Jets"—jets as in jetsetter. Rebecca called me by the nickname, too, which sounded precious with her lisp.

There's no question that Paige was proud of my accomplishments, but her real priority was finding a rich man to take care of me. Whenever we were out together and she spotted an attractive young man, she'd grab me and hiss in my ear, "Geri, check that one out! When I was your age, what I wouldn't do to him!"

"Paige, that's just not my style," I told her time and time again. But Paige was determined. She repeatedly set me up with guys I had no interest in, based on their fat bank accounts alone. She even flew a guy in from Miami once to meet me, a bona fide multimillionaire who looked just like Lurch from *The Addams Family.*

"Paige, are you out of your mind?" I asked her.

"Geri, he's a *millionaire*," she reminded me.

"That doesn't matter to me," I protested. "I'm waiting for the right guy. Plus, I need to focus on my career."

I meant what I said. Unfortunately, shortly thereafter, Tower Dresses folded, and I found myself out of a job for the first time. At twenty-one years old, I was collecting unemployment, standing in line with people twice my age who had mortgages to pay and children to support. Around that time, my cousin's father remarried and had a baby named Megan. Since Megan's mom, Linda, liked to work out most mornings, they hired me to watch the baby from 7:30 a.m. until about noon on weekdays. Weekends, I looked after Rebecca, and the rest of my time I spent going on interviews and trying to find a "real" job.

Being a child at heart, I loved spending time with kids. But as time went on and I couldn't find a position in my field, I started to get discouraged. Paige and Stan were getting ready to make their annual summer pilgrimage to Italy, and Paige decided I should join them.

"Come on, Jets," she said. "You need a break from the stress of job hunting. We're going to go all over Italy. There's going to be gorgeous men everywhere. You'll have the time of your life."

My mother was dead set against the idea.

"You can't be running off to Italy when you need to find a job!" she yelled. "What do you think, life is some big party?"

Her objections didn't make sense, because I wasn't just getting a free trip to Italy, I would be getting paid for it: a thousand dollars for twenty-one days. Plus, I wouldn't have to pay for any of my meals, and Paige and Stan said I could have nights to myself after Rebecca went to sleep (which was fairly early, considering she was only five). It was going to be a grand tour of my ancestors' homeland—Grandma Rosaria was from Abruzzi, and my grandfather was from Naples. We'd be visiting Stresa, the lake region, Milan, Rome, and Venice—and that last one was the best part, because we'd be staying at The Gritti Palace, which dated back to the fourteenth century and was located right across from the Grand Canal. I'd have my own room, which probably went for about twelve hundred dollars a night—and we'd be there for two solid weeks.

The trip was, indeed, magical. The Gritti Palace was close to Piazza San Marco—Saint Mark's Square—that famously pigeon-filled spot seen in so many movies. There were shops selling the most exquisite jewelry and handblown glass I'd ever seen. Stan was a friend of the owner of the exclusive Nardi jewelry boutique, and he always bought Paige a unique piece on their annual trip.

Stan and Paige could fit in anywhere, and Stan had been visiting Italy since he was a boy trailing after his father. He knew the scene, and he had long friendships with Italian families, who would invite us to their homes and feed us. They just loved to love. I was an American Italian, and I felt like I was family.

While we were at The Gritti Palace, other notable guests included Pia Zadora, Tom Hanks, Rita Wilson, and Siegfried and Roy. Prince Andrew and Fergie passed by us on their boat. Mel Brooks and Anne Bancroft's cabana was just a stone's throw away from ours at Lido Beach, where Rebecca and I spent hours every day being spoiled rotten by cabana boys, who would fetch us towels, grapes, anything we needed.

Sometimes I would exercise on the beach with Paige before Rebecca and Stan woke up in the morning. Mel Brooks was always up early too, and he'd look at the topless bathers before his wife, Anne, arose. Paige always went topless, but I couldn't bring myself to do more than slide my bathing suit straps off my shoulders. Inevitably, we'd be lying on our cots after our workout when Mel Brooks walked by, and he would call out to us, "Good morning, ladies!"

I would keep my arms crossed over my chest, and we'd return the greeting.

On our last day, when we saw him approaching as usual, Paige said to me, "Oh, why don't you just give him a peek." So, I threw my towel aside, sat up, and yelled, "Good morning, Mr. Brooks!"

He looked a bit startled, but he didn't miss a beat. "Good *morning*, ladies!" he replied with a leer in his voice.

I was outgoing by nature, and it wasn't that I didn't like to flirt—I did. But I was never flirtatious simply for the sake of being flirtatious. Still, Paige was always pushing me to be sexier than I felt comfortable with. When I came back from Jet Skiing with the lifeguards, she would say, "Oooh, those lifeguards got the hots for Jets!" She said the same thing about the young men who sold fresh fish and roasted eggplant, or *melanzana*, at the beach snack stands. (No greasy burgers or hot dogs in Venice's Lido Beach!)

Part of me liked it, I'll admit. I definitely felt the pull of the "bad angel" on my shoulder from time to time. Here I was, an attractive, young, single woman in Venice, surrounded by intriguing men and potential sugar daddies. Another girl in my place might have behaved very differently. But I was still a good Catholic girl from Westchester at heart, and I felt a responsibility to be a good role model for Rebecca. Stan and Paige were wonderful parents, but they were living in a world most people can only dream of. If Rebecca wanted a horse, for example, she would most likely get a horse. Because I was coming from such a different place, I believed it was part of my job to help teach Rebecca about the value of people and life. Throwing myself at wealthy European men was no way to do that, I was sure.

Then there was the issue of Rebecca not exactly wanting her beloved Geri Jets to pay attention to anyone else. She became more and more possessive of me the more time we spent together. But I didn't mind. Everyone recognized us in the square.

"Signorita, I want to go out with your babysitter!" The gondolier guys would call out.

"No way, José!" Rebecca would yell back.

Sometimes, she would tell prospective suitors that they had to pass a quiz in order to take me out on a date. "What color is the sky?" she would ask.

The guys would inevitably say *blue*.

"What color is the grass?"

The guys would say *green*.

"What color is the ocean?" she would ask.

This one was something of a trick question, the guys would point out, since the Adriatic Sea is both blue and green.

She would tell them to pick one. Her final question, however, was the real trick question.

"What was the first question I asked you?" she would say, her eyes filling with mischief.

"What color is the sky," the guys would answer.

But they were wrong, as Rebecca would gleefully

inform them: the first question she asked was "Do you want to take a quiz?" So no one ever, ever passed. Not that I minded; on the contrary, the whole thing made me laugh (and made me grateful to have an excuse to get away from those hopeful Casanovas).

One evening, Paige and Stan were out for dinner, and Rebecca and I got dressed up—she wore jeweled clip-on earrings and little bit of my makeup—and we went to a popular Venetian bistro, where the staff knew us. Rebecca ordered a hamburger and fries in Italian, and I ordered Venetian liver. Suddenly, the other patrons began clapping. We looked around and spotted a man down on one knee, proposing marriage to his dinner companion.

Rebecca loved the glittering ring he held out. "I want that ring," she whispered to me.

"Well," I said, "go ask them. Just be polite."

So, she went over and said, "Excuse me. What a pretty ring. Can I have it?"

The man smiled. "I'm sorry, but this is a special day and a special ring," he said. "But . . . what were you thinking of trading?"

Rebecca ran back to me. "What should I offer him?"

I suggested our silverware. Rebecca went back with that offer, but the man declined. So, she upped the ante to an entire place setting. Still, it was no deal. Then, she smiled at me and went into the kitchen, trailed by the maître d'. When she came back, she had the chef in his tall white hat by the hand. She led him to the couple's table, and said, "I'll throw in the chef!"

The chef bowed deeply, and the whole restaurant

erupted in laughter. After dinner, Rebecca and I went dancing in Saint Mark's Square.

Paige and I had a deal: I put Rebecca in bed around nine o'clock, and after that I was free to do whatever I wanted. Except, the sun was just going down around nine, so Rebecca was never quite ready to call it a day at that hour (especially because she usually recharged with a late-afternoon, post-beach siesta, as is customary in Italy). So, by the time her eyes closed for good, it was more like ten o'clock—at which point my own eyes were getting pretty heavy after running around on the hot beach all day. It was tempting to just sink into the luxurious bedding in my beautiful hotel room and fall into a deep sleep, but I pushed myself to go out and seize the day (or night). This was a once-in-a-lifetime opportunity, I reminded myself.

* * *

One afternoon, as Paige and I made our way home from the beach with Rebecca, we stopped at our usual deli for a late-afternoon lunch of prosciutto, olives, fresh bread, and cheese, which we would take back to the hotel and enjoy with a glass of wine on our veranda. They were all foods I grew up eating, but everything tasted so much better in Italy, especially in the salt air. (I still dream about that cheese—Bel Paese, which means "beautiful country," and was eaten at room temperature, making the flavors dance on your tongue.) I thought I was in heaven!

After we picked up our savory goodies, Rebecca

wanted ice cream. Paige said okay, so we stopped by the gelato stand. Two young Italian men were standing there, watching the owner scooping gelato into cones and cups for all the hot and hungry beachgoers. Both young men were good-looking, but the shorter of the two had an especially handsome face with very kind eyes. Paige spoke to them in her New York Jewish–accented Italian, but I couldn't understand a word. Even though I grew up around my grandmother speaking Italian, my mother never learned it, so my brothers and I ended up with only a very basic knowledge of the language—just a few key words and phrases.

Still, I felt comfortable when people were speaking Italian around me, and I was not entirely in the dark. Even if I couldn't comprehend exactly what was being said, I picked up on the general idea of what the conversation was about. So, I knew that these guys were asking Paige about me. I also got that they were in the army (in Italy, it was mandatory for boys to spend two years in the service after high school). I pulled out my pocket English-to-Italian dictionary and tried to join the conversation. The shorter, handsome one pulled out his driver's license to show me his name—Thomas. So, I did the same. Our eyes met in shock. We had the exact same birthdate: March 12, 1965. It had to be a sign! I wanted to keep talking, but Paige was anxious to get going.

"Come on Jets, tell them you'll meet them another night after you put Becca to bed," she said.

Paige helped me to plan a meeting with Thomas at the clock tower in Saint Mark's Square—not the next night, but the night after. I remember pointing at the word *Wednesday* in my little dictionary.

As Paige pulled me away, she rolled her eyes. "What am I going to do with you?" she asked in a loud whisper. "Making plans with some broke kid in the army when I'm trying to set you up with millionaires!"

"None of the millionaires are as cute as Thomas," I pointed out.

When Wednesday night rolled around, I couldn't wait for Rebecca to get to sleep. She was all tucked into her bed, and I was lying in the single bed on the other side of the nightstand. What Rebecca didn't know was that underneath the covers, I was fully dressed. I chose a slim taupe skirt and button-down knit top for the occasion; I was even wearing eyeliner, which I usually did not. (It was fashionable, but secretly, I thought it made me look cross-eyed.)

"Jets, I can't fall asleep if you don't tell me a story," Rebecca called from her bed.

Stories had become our bedtime routine. Sometimes I would use our day as inspiration, exaggerating what really happened to turn it into an exciting adventure. Other times I would tell her a true story from my childhood. On that evening, that's what Rebecca wanted to hear.

"I want the spider story!" she said.

The spider story, as we called it, was one of her favorites. It was a longer one than I felt like telling, honestly, but I figured it would tire her out. And it might distract me from the pre-date butterflies beginning to flutter in my stomach. By the end of the tale (a true account of a giant spider my little brother and I once caught), Rebecca's eyes were finally starting to droop.

"Jets, can you tell me another story?"

"That's plenty for tonight, Becca," I said.

I had ten minutes to get to the clock tower in Saint Mark's Square. I told Rebecca that I was going to the bathroom and never went back—she was fast asleep within seconds anyway. Luckily, I didn't have far to go, and I knew how to get there. Stan had clued me in that the bricks in the sidewalks pointed toward Saint Mark's Square, saying that if I ever got lost, all I had to do was follow the bricks. So, I just looked at the ground and ran.

When I got to the square, it was filled with tourists and locals alike, sipping espresso and indulging in gelato. Kids were chasing each other around, dancing to a live orchestra that moved from one side of the square to the other. Since the sun had gone down, the pigeons were absent for the time being.

It was a spectacular night—clear, warm, with a sky full of stars. I wanted to share it with someone, but there was nobody around. I made my way to the clock tower, which dated back to the fifteenth century and featured two huge bronze figures that would strike the hour on a bell. The bell hadn't chimed yet, so I knew I wasn't late. I straightened my skirt and fiddled with the eighteen-karat gold bracelet from Nardi's that Stan had given me as a gift. I hoped I wasn't sweating too much and said a little prayer to my guardian angel. Looking up at the magnificent art-filled sky, I instantly felt protected.

Suddenly, across the square, I spotted a man. It wasn't Thomas; this man looked older and more sophisticated. He had what I would call a confident beauty about him. He wore loose-fitting slacks and sandals and a soft-looking shirt with several buttons undone, all in neutrals. His hair was on the longer side, falling a little below his chin, and his eyes were bright blue. He looked like an angel. He reminded me of an Italian Kurt Russell. He was with a small group of equally beautiful, well-dressed people. Nothing they wore matched, exactly, but every piece complemented the others perfectly. Italy was where I truly learned the importance of quality over quantity. Italians didn't care if they wore the same shirt three days in a row if it was their best shirt. Dressing in one's best clothes was a sign of respect for others, and they were always presenting their best selves. The way they interacted with each other showed a level of respect I wasn't used to seeing, too. They were kind and affectionate with each other, but not in a forced way. As the bells chimed, I watched them wistfully and wondered if Thomas was ever going to show up. I was starting to feel like people were staring at me.

Then, as I tried not to stare, the Italian Kurt Russell started walking toward me across the square. He stopped and smiled when he got to my side.

"*Buona sera*," he said, and then switched to English. "What is your name?"

"Geraldine," I answered, smiling back.

"Ah, Geraldina," he said. "My name is Angelo. What are you doing, waiting for some army boys to show up?

Come and join me and my friends."

I laughed. How did he know? Was I that much of a cliché? I was intimidated. I didn't speak Italian.

"Where are you from?" Angelo asked.

"New York," I told him.

"A beautiful girl from New York is going to stand under a clock tower and wait for an army boy? Come with me. *Andiamo*!"

I wasn't sure what to do. On one hand, Angelo's offer was extremely attractive . . . and so was he. On the other, it was only a few minutes past ten o'clock, and I felt an obligation to Thomas.

"I'll give you a few minutes to think about it," Angelo said graciously, and he sauntered back to his friends. I noticed that they weren't talking about me or even looking at me—it was so different from the way it was in the States, where you could always tell that a guy's friends were sizing you up.

At this point, Thomas was definitely late. I could hear my mother's voice in my head: *Be smart. Go back to the hotel and go to bed. What girl in her right mind would go out with a perfect stranger in a country where she didn't even speak the language?*

Angelo was already walking back toward me. I looked at those blue eyes, and my pulse started racing.

"So, Geraldina," he said. "What did you decide?"

I paused. Something was still holding me back, and he could sense it.

"Maybe my friends are too much?" he suggested. "Perhaps you would feel better if it was just you and me?"

"Just you and me," I blurted. I don't even know why I said it.

But Angelo didn't second guess me. He turned around and said "ciao" to each of his friends by name; all of them waved back and included me in their good-byes: "Ciao, Angelo and Geraldina!"

Angelo took me by the arm and led me away from the square. "I want to take you to a very nice café," he said. "But to get there, we have to take the vaporetto."

The vaporetto was a waterbus, the Venetian version of public transportation. It was often crowded and bumpy, but I figured at least we'd be surrounded by a lot of witnesses if Angelo turned out to be a psycho and tried to push me overboard. He was a complete stranger, after all.

The moon was coming up over the Grand Canal as we boarded the boat. Another man who looked to be around my age approached us, greeting Angelo. Angelo excused himself for a moment and went over to talk. As the two young men caught up with each other, I could see that Angelo maybe wasn't quite as sophisticated as he seemed at first. His youth was showing, to put it simply. Something else was showing, too, though. Angelo put his hand on his friend's shoulder, lowering his head to speak close to his friend's ear, and I saw a look of compassion on his face that was even better than sophistication.

Angelo brought the man over to me and introduced us. His wife was sick, Angelo explained to me, and he'd invited him to have a drink with us. We got a table at a café, and I sipped a Campari and soda with an orange twist while Angelo and his friend talked. Angelo tried to include me in the conversation as much as possible, even though his friend didn't speak English, but I didn't mind being quiet. I'd never had Campari before, and it had been a long time since I'd had anything to eat. I was starting to feel lightheaded.

Fortunately, Angelo's friend needed to leave, so we were free to go and get something to eat. Unfortunately, I had a glass of wine with our meal, so my lightheadedness did not go away. Still, I was just so in awe of what was happening to me at that moment that I didn't care. Here I was in Venice, having dinner with a handsome stranger. It was just unbelievable.

After we finished our meal, Angelo took me by the hand again and led me to where the locals had their beach cabanas. They weren't anywhere near as luxurious as the cabanas at the resort, where even the canvas of the awnings was of better quality, but they were still lovely. And they were an absolutely perfect spot for a twenty-something girl from New York to kiss a mysterious Italian heartthrob. Angelo and I had chemistry, that much I knew.

Between the silvery stars scattered across the night sky and the bright white moon reflected in the velvety black waves, it would have been a postcard-perfect memory even without the chemistry, to be honest. As for how much chemistry we truly had, it was hard to tell . . . I was feeling woozy.

"Let me take you back," Angelo offered. He was a perfect gentleman, steering me through the crowd to the vaporetto protectively. At first, I thought I should sit inside the boat's cabin on one of the bright-red vinyl benches. But soon it became apparent that I needed fresh air. I was outside on the deck, bent over the railing, when I finally got sick. I was so embarrassed, but Angelo was very sweet. "Hey, it happens," he said, shrugging.

I felt much better after my stomach was empty, but I was still ready to call it a night. And even though I was just about convinced that Angelo was genuinely a nice person by then, I was still a bit wary of letting him walk me back to the hotel. Maybe I'd seen too many suspense movies, but what if he was a jewel thief just trying to get to Paige's valuables through me?

"Please, let me walk you back," Angelo said. "I'm worried about you."

I reluctantly agreed, and we strolled slowly back to The Gritti. At the boat landing in front of the hotel, we sat and had a coffee while gazing out at the magnificently flowerbeds, glowing in the light of the moon. The breeze on the water made a soft rippling noise. It was like a fairy tale.

Angelo and I made plans to meet again, and this time, I'd introduce him to Paige and Stan.

* * *

"Paige, he is *so* handsome!" I said the next morning, still riding high from being with Angelo.

"I'm telling you Jets, you better be careful," Paige said. "If he's so beautiful, he could be some kind of gigolo. What if he's a jewelry thief?"

"Oh my God," I said. "That was the first thing I thought!" Paige and I must have been watching the same movies.

Paige tried to convince Stan that he should ask around about Angelo and try to dig up some dirt, but Stan only rolled his eyes. "Will you leave Geri alone and let her have a good time?"

I needed Paige's help, though, to confirm my next date with Angelo. Since I only knew a few words in Italian, I was afraid to call his house, so I asked Paige to do it. Angelo's mother answered, and Paige asked to speak with Angelo. The next thing we knew, his mother was screaming in Italian.

It turned out that Angelo was named after his father, and she thought some strange woman was calling to speak to her husband!

"Tell her it's for her son, her son!" I whispered to Paige.

Paige and Stan made an exception to their rule about me only going out after Rebecca went to sleep so I could visit Angelo at his home during daylight hours. That date was unlike the first. Instead of being shown around one of the most magical cities in Europe by a good-looking foreigner, I was just making out with a hot young guy in his bedroom at his mother's house. It was like being back in high school, but not in a bad way. We were getting to know each other as real people, moving past the intrigue of our different backgrounds.

After a long kiss, Angelo pulled away to look at me. A sort of shyness came over him.

"I have to be honest with you," he said.

Here it comes, I thought. He really is a jewelry thief. Angelo took a deep breath.

"I'm a model," he said.

The first thing I felt was relief. Then the marketing girl in me took over. "You need to come to the States!" I said. "You're so beautiful, you could have a huge career."

"You really think so?" I could tell that Angelo was excited to hear a girl from New York say she thought he had a real chance. He jumped up and pulled a photo album out of his closet. It was filled with pictures of Angelo posing next to beautiful Italian women. Quickly, it dawned on me: Angelo wasn't just a model; he was an escort—an escort looking to break out and move into the legitimate fashion world full time.

This realization made me worry, for a moment, that Angelo's only intention had been to use me as a ticket to America. But even if that had been his sole motive, hadn't I been fantasizing, too? About moving to Italy for the perfect man.

As much as his life looked like a fairy tale to me, the reality was that Angelo felt trapped by his limited opportunities in Venice. He wanted more than he had. Meanwhile, I wanted the real deal. I had always gotten along well with men, probably because I had two brothers, yet I never had a boyfriend in high school. (In fact, I'd gone to five high school proms with guys who were just friends!) In my imagination, I'd been spinning a mere attraction to Angelo into a real relationship.

We were both figuring out who we were and day-dreaming about realities we didn't have. We were both judging books by their covers.

The fact that Thomas and I shared the same birth date wasn't a sign that we were meant to be together, either. I was looking for signs that fit a plan that I'd imagined for myself; I had not yet begun to fully trust God to lead me. And, as I would discover, He doesn't always send the signs we expect in the way we think they'll arrive.

Chapter Five

The Cost of Freedom

As is often the case when young adults get their first taste of real independence and the great, wide world beyond the surroundings in which they grew up, I came home from Italy with a new kind of confidence and a sense of purpose. Unfortunately, none of that changed the fact that I was still unemployed, but it probably helped me land my next job, which was at a Nine West store in the Galleria Mall in White Plains, New York.

I didn't want to be a cashier selling shoes, but once again, Mrs. Lentz had given me the tip, and I trusted my mentor. "Look," she'd said, "These guys are hot. They're up and coming. You could grow with Nine West."

My boss there, a man named Elio, just happened to speak with a heavy Italian accent—a small detail, perhaps, but one that nevertheless felt like something of a sign. There must have been something about me that felt like a good omen to Elio, too, because he took me under his wing in a way that not only made my experience as his employee more valuable but also taught me about leadership. Elio was kind to me, but he never settled for less than my absolute best. Eventually, I got promoted to assistant store manager at the Nine West store in the Stamford Town Center mall in Connecticut. When I left for Stamford, Elio sent me a note.

Another boss might have simply signed a congratulatory card. Not Elio. He included a warning of sorts. According to him, I'd lived something of a sheltered existence and needed to experience some kind of trauma or struggle in order to understand the true meaning of life.

Elio's words stayed with me. What exactly was he talking about? In a sense, he was right; I did have a great childhood, and good things had happened to me for most of my life. At the same time, everyone struggles. Every family has problems, my own included. I hadn't been so sheltered that I couldn't understand the meaning of life, had I?

* * *

Stamford Town Center was a shorter commute from my parents' home, where I was still living, but I'd recently had a falling out with my mother. She'd finally decided to use the $250 Fendi leather handbag I brought home from Italy for her. For months, she hadn't touched the bag, so I'd started using it myself. (No way I was going to see that gorgeous purse go to waste!) When she finally went to put her own wallet and tissues and whatever else inside the bag, she had to remove my belongings first, and those belongings included birth control pills.

I was dating a guy named Daniel at the time. He was sweet and funny and athletic and good-looking (and totally in love with me), but he wasn't particularly ambitious. I dominated the relationship but didn't necessarily relish that position; I certainly couldn't see starting my career with Daniel at my side, never mind having a child with him. I was being responsible by taking the birth control pills, but in my mother's opinion, having sex outside of marriage was a sin. Period.

Mom discovered the pills on the Friday evening that Daniel and I planned to drive to Cape Cod for the weekend. Mom summoned Dad upstairs for a meeting and told the boys to stay downstairs. She was furious.

"What are we going to do about this?" she asked Dad, showing him what she'd found.

Meanwhile, my older brother was out in the driveway telling Daniel that he didn't know what was going on in the house, but Daniel had better drive around the block a few times before coming in to pick me up.

Dad stood up for me. "Teresa," he said, "she's a good girl. She's doing the responsible thing."

"*What?*" Mom was now as angry with him as she was with me.

I don't know how he calmed her down, because I went to Cape Cod as planned. In my heart, I knew I was doing the right thing by preventing a pregnancy. But I felt so much shame as a result of my mother's reaction to finding the pills that I stopped taking them altogether. It didn't matter, anyway, as I ended up breaking up with Daniel.

My boss in Stamford was a woman related to the Florsheim Shoes family. She may have known shoes, but she was a terrible manager. Her salespeople were stealing, and she set people up to fail. One time, she went on vacation after grossly overordering shoes, and we had no place to put them when they were delivered. I felt sorry for the whole staff. I called senior management and said, "You'd better get down here and see this."

My manager's values and mine were at odds, and I knew that I should move on. But senior management asked me to stay in Stamford and spy on my boss—just keep some notes.

I said no.

They said, "Hang tight, then."

Soon enough, I was promoted and sent to open the first Long Island store at the Smith Haven Mall in Lake Grove, way out on Long Island. That meant moving out of my parents' house—freedom at last!

My mother and I had clashed again, this time, over a magazine cover. It depicted a sophisticated-looking woman in a pencil skirt, stepping out of a cab. When I looked at that photo, I saw an independent business-woman, the encapsulation of one of my dreams for my-self. My mother, who was married at twenty-three and a mom soon after, saw something different. "Don't get caught up in the image," she said. "People aren't really like that."

The generational divide was frustrating. I loved my mother, but I loved being rewarded for my hard work, too. I'd seen extremely successful women at work in the Garment District, and I wanted that kind of success. I was inching toward the person I wanted to be.

My freedom was unique among my friends. They

were still in college, and I was finished with school. I will never forget the day I drove to Stonybrook—my first home away from home. I was a businesswoman in charge of a million-dollar business. I was on my way to "making it" in the real world. The grace of adulthood was mine. With the sun roof and all the windows open, the wind blowing in my face, and the stereo blaring, I went hoarse singing along with Long Island's own piano man, Billy Joel.

This is what independence feels like, I thought. I was twenty-three years old.

* * *

At the Nine West in the Smith Haven Mall, most of my staff members were younger than I was. As Elio had been to me, I became a mentor for them, and we sometimes socialized after work. The drinking age in New York had just been raised to twenty-one, which left me with only a handful of employees who could meet for the occasional drink, and I didn't really know anyone else in the area. When I had the courage to dine out by myself, I went to a cute bar and restaurant about a half a mile from my house called the Country House. It featured live music, and I would linger after my meal to dance, hoping maybe I would meet somebody interesting.

One night, my wish came true. Lucas had a slight physique, dark hair and dark eyes, and a look that reminded me a bit of the men in Italy (in fact, he was from Spain). When he asked me to dance, I said yes without hesitating. It was so nice to have someone to dance with . . . and Lucas danced well, too. At the end of that night, we kissed, and Lucas asked for my number. I gave it to him without hesitation.

Lucas liked photography, and he would take me (and his camera) to the most scenic places around Long Island for mini photo shoots. So much of the time when we were together, things were joyful. But Lucas was divorced, with two children. He'd been living in the basement of his father's house since he and his wife split up. There was something dark about him, something I blamed on his circumstances, though it might have gone deeper than that. But he called regularly, and when we made a plan, he stuck to it. No games.

We couldn't do much because he never had extra money, but that was okay, because I was working anywhere from fifty to seventy hours a week. When I had time off, I just looked forward to relaxing with Lucas. I was working hard and paying my bills on time. I loved living on my own. I knew Lucas didn't love me and that I deserved more. But we did have chemistry, and I was lonely.

One night when I visited him in his basement apartment, we ended up in bed. I had mittelschmerz (pain in the lower abdomen at the time of ovulation), a term defined by one of my friends as "the evil ovary." It didn't occur every month, and one month it would be on my left side and then a few months later, it would be on my right side. The discomfort didn't last long, but it was nature's way of letting me know I was in the middle of my cycle. So, I told him to pull out—but he didn't.

I froze. I hadn't taken the pill since my mother discovered my birth control stash. And immediately, I knew. "I'm pregnant," I yelled, jumping out of his bed.

Lucas looked at me like I was an idiot and laughed, and then he got up and sauntered outside to smoke a cigarette.

When I met Lucas, I'd thought that maybe God's plan for me was to become an instant mom—a stepmother to his children. But now I knew Lucas was not the right man for me. His aloofness in the face of my fear and his lack of concern were evidence of that. He didn't say, "I shouldn't have done that; I'm sorry." *He laughed at me.* He'd been looking for sex, I realized; not love.

How could I have been so naïve? How could I have gotten myself into this mess?

I was panicked at the thought of what my mother would say. If I had stayed on the pill, this wouldn't have happened, and this was far worse.

I knew what her first thought would be: that this was somehow her fault, and that was wrong. It was one hundred percent *my* fault for having unprotected sex. For having sex before marriage. I was disgusted with myself for what I'd done. But I knew she'd blame herself anyway, and the prospect of that filled me with such guilt and dread that I knew I could not tell her, ever.

I was furious with Lucas for his vulgar disregard. I was ashamed of him—no, I was ashamed of myself. He was divorced with two kids! What would my parents think? Why hadn't I thought it through before sleeping with him? I'd put myself in this bind, and the little girl in me desperately wanted to extricate myself without letting my parents down. Everything in me wanted to pretend this accident never happened. Though my parents had married young, their union was full of love, and it provided me with a strong role model for marriage. I could never bring life into this world without the kind of love they had.

I always knew my body well, and my periods were regular. The minute my period was late (and I mean I counted the actual minutes), I took the pregnancy test. The world stopped when I saw that line. But not for long. I'd already made the decision, and I had numbed myself to it.

One of my best friends drove from Westchester to accompany me to the procedure, which I had done as soon as medically possible. It was as if it were happening to someone else. She sat and wished she could take away my grief. No one could. She sat quiet, prayerful and steadfast until it was time to go home.

I never saw Lucas again, even from a distance. I went to church and confessed my sins, but even that didn't dull the guilt and remorse I felt. I wished I could talk to my mother about it, but that was impossible. So, I stopped talking about it to myself, too. I stuffed the disgust and guilt and remorse deep inside, where it slowly began to eat a hole in my soul.

Chapter Six

Missed My Calling

The Nine West company was planning to open a store in the Roosevelt Field Mall in Garden City, New York, which is still on Long Island, but closer to Manhattan. Roosevelt Field was a dynamo among malls. It was close enough to John F. Kennedy and LaGuardia international airports to attract airline passengers and flight attendants on layover, and its revenue per square foot was double the national average. I was asked to manage the new Nine West store.

I moved into a house share with a woman named Brianna. She worked for IBM and dressed like a *Vogue* cover model, but she was a slovenly housekeeper. If the phone rang, we'd have to find it by following the cord, and inevitably, it was under a pile of clothing on her bedroom floor. One day, she called me in a panic. Her European boyfriend Ivan was coming that day for a visit, and her room was a mess. I advised her to invest in some heavy-duty black Hefty bags and move all her stuff to the garage. When I got home that evening, she'd not only followed my advice; she'd also redecorated the house and bought a Laura Ashley sofa and loveseat for the living room. Brianna was crazy, but she was also funny and smart and seldom at home.

I spent my days off working on my tan at Robert Moses State Park, the beach next to Fire Island. At work, I was doing extremely well. The store's sales exceeded the expectations of the owners: Vince Camuto, the style man, and Jack Fisher, the numbers man. They would visit the store, and Mr. Fisher would take me out for ice cream. We'd walk around the mall, and he'd pick my brain about floor displays, consumer shopping habits, and what styles were hot. My sales numbers were beating those at the company's flagship store on West Fifty-Seventh Street in New York City. I'd been with Nine West for six years by then, and I was interested in moving into a nonsales role at the corporate offices, which were in Stamford then but eventually were moved to 111 Westchester Avenue in Westchester, New York.

It was customary for mall tenants to negotiate a rental amount with a double-sided caveat: if sales were lower than expected, the tenant could leave without penalty. But if sales exceeded expectations, the tenant paid additional rent of 6 percent of the "overage." My store was an overage tenant, and the mall's general manager named me president of the merchants' association because I was such a good role model. I finally felt like the woman in the pencil skirt on the magazine cover. I was on my way.

The Nine West company was a major sponsor of the nonprofit Ms. Foundation for Women, of which Gloria Steinem and Marlo Thomas were among the "founding mothers," and Ms. was launching its first annual Take Your Daughter to Work Day to encourage girls to think about careers. The Roosevelt Field general manager asked me to manage the event for the whole mall.

My team gathered influential businesswomen throughout the community. We invited elected officials and the media. Actress Kathy Najimy, who appeared with Whoopi Goldberg in *Sister Act*, was keynote speaker. I invited my regional vice president, Gina Burns, to come. If she sees me in action, I thought, she might recommend me for promotion to the corporate office.

The day was a smashing success. By the end of our panel discussion, however, the girls in the audience, just five to twelve years old, were beginning to wilt. They were tired and restless. When I got up to thank everyone for participating, I asked the children to stand up and stretch their arms to the ceiling. I asked if they'd had a good time and what they liked best and what they liked least. Then I asked them to sit, and I spoke to the parents. To help their daughters identify the careers they'll excel in, I said, "Have them create a résumé for life. Each year, have them write down what they are good at and what they really love to do, and save those findings in an envelope. Documenting their interests will show them that their interests are important and may very well point them toward a satisfying career when they are older."

When I finished speaking, Kathy Najimy, said, "You had that audience mesmerized! Have you ever considered acting?"

That's funny, I thought. I wasn't acting; I was being myself. I was speaking from my heart. To be a good employee takes dedication and hard work and loving what you do makes work easier.

Then Gina Burns came over to me and said, "Geri, you were just amazing. You had everyone's attention— the reporters, the TV crews, the kids, their parents, and the panel." She paused for a moment, and then added: "It's a shame you missed your calling."

She'd meant it as a compliment, but that comment was a life changer. I had a revelation at that moment: it was time for me to move on. Gina apparently did not see me in a corporate role. She didn't really see me at all. "I haven't missed my calling," I said. "I've just begun." Then, with my heart racing, I added, "I'm giving you six weeks' notice. I'm resigning from Nine West."

Gina was dumbfounded. Her face grew beet red. "Well, we do need to do your review," she said.

"There's no need for a review," I said. "I've been here since 6:30 this morning. I'm going home. Have a good evening." Blood was pounding in my ears as I turned and walked away, but I felt alive. I was honoring my intuition.

The general manager of Roosevelt Field had often asked me, "What are you doing selling shoes when you could run this place?" So, the day after resigning my shoe-selling job, I asked him how I could get involved in the mall business. He told me to drop my résumé in his office, and he would pass it on to a colleague who worked for General Growth Properties, a mall developer based in the Midwest. Before I knew it, I was flying to Minneapolis to interview for a marketing position at one of GGP's malls.

The first of the five executives I met with that day put to rest my fear that I didn't have the right credentials for upper management. He glanced at my résumé, which showed that I had an associate's degree and not the bachelor's degree required for the position that was open. Then he crumpled it up and tossed it like a basketball into the trash can. "Tell me about yourself," he said.

GGP hired me to be marketing director for the Granite Run Mall in Media, Pennsylvania. Almost immediately, I was flown to Palm Springs, California, for a corporate meeting. It was held at the hotel where singer-turned-politician Sonny Bono owned a restaurant called Bono's. Each conference attendee was given a plush bathrobe with a big star on the lapel. STARS—Steps to Achieve Real Success—was the theme of the conference, and we were told that we were GGP's stars. I was dazzled by how people-centered GGP seemed to be, and I was ready to give the company my all.

Chapter Seven

The Bride Whisperer

While my own personal life often felt like an endless series of stops and starts, everywhere I walked, love bloomed like flowers in my footsteps . . . for other people. It wasn't so much that I was a matchmaker; it's more like I was some kind of enchanted wing woman whose presence all but guaranteed that the single lady in my company would find her soul mate. Honestly, I should have called myself the Bride Whisperer.

My romantic Midas touch went all the way back to high school. Liz was a blonde-haired, blue-eyed Southern girl who didn't know anyone when she moved to Westchester and joined my class at school. Being the naturally outgoing and maternal type, I automatically took her under my wing and introduced her to everyone I knew. In the process, we became close friends. Even though Liz was Protestant and I was Catholic, we both came from families centered on faith. Liz was sweet and good-natured and fun to be around. But there was also a sadness to her that she couldn't seem to shake. She was always down on herself about everything, especially her appearance, which I could never understand. Secretly, I suspected she was bulimic. So, I was always trying to figure out ways to cheer her up.

After we graduated high school, that usually involved going out dancing all night. I was always the designated driver, but I still managed to have a blast. On one such occasion, Liz and I were at 21 North in New Rochelle, a hotspot that attracted people from all five boroughs of New York City. Liz was feeling particularly depressed and had a little too much to drink. The combination of booze and a bad mood resulted in her having a mini breakdown, sobbing to me at the club that she was never going to find the right guy. The last thing she needed at that moment, I decided, was to be surrounded by loud music and flirting couples.

"Let's get you out of here," I said. "Come on, we need to put gas in the car anyway."

We left our girlfriends behind in the club, and I led Liz tottering out into the fresh air.

"Liz, you're such a beautiful girl," I told her as we drove to the gas station down the street. "You just have to believe in yourself."

"I just feel like nothing good is ever going to happen for me," she said. Her voice was trembling, but I could see in her eyes that my words were what she needed to hear at that moment. People like Liz respond to kindness, I've learned, because they don't know how to be kind to themselves.

When we got to the service station, I sent Liz into the convenience store to pick up some Diet Coke and pretzels. A little caffeine and starch to soak up the alcohol would do her good. As I was filling my car with gas, a cute little sports car pulled up to the adjacent pump with two very attractive men inside. I noticed them, naturally, but didn't go out of my way to make eye contact. It was the middle of the night on a Saturday—odds were these two guys were out on the prowl looking for a good time and not much else. But I watched as one of them (the more handsome of the two) went into the convenience store where Liz was paying for the pretzels and soda. Through the window, I could see him approach my friend. The two of them exchanged some words, and Liz laughed. I hadn't seen her face light up like that in a long time. From her reaction, I could tell that he wasn't being sleazy or giving her the usual tacky pickup lines you'd expect to hear in that kind of situation. It looked like they were having a real conversation. From out of nowhere, these words popped into my head: "She's going to marry him." Right away, I had to laugh at myself. What would make me think that Liz would end up marrying some guy she met after midnight at a gas station?

I watched as Liz waved good-bye to the stranger, who headed back to the sports car. I could tell that she was trying to act cool while he was still around, but the way she came running over told me something big was going on.

"Geri, oh my gosh! That guy was so cute!" Liz was out of breath. "His name is Matt. He asked me out to brunch on Sunday!"

"He looked like a really nice guy," I told her, and I meant it.

I was right, too. Matt was a nice guy. So nice, in fact,

that Liz married him, had a beautiful family of daughters, and lived happily ever after in Yorktown. I was the maid of honor at their wedding.

Liz was far from the only one of my friends to meet the man of her dreams on my watch. It happened so often that I started keeping a record.

My girlfriend Kim's path to marriage started out with another night at a club and a conversation like the one I'd had with Liz. We were at Electric Rain when I introduced her to a nice-looking man named Rob. He and I had been friendly with one another in high school, and a lot of girls had secret crushes on him. I thought he was a good person and perfect for Kimby Mac—short for McIntyre—which was my nickname for her. Again, I knew I'd been right when I was the maid of honor at their wedding!

My girlfriends and I loved to dance, and of course we were on the lookout for the perfect men for us. But truth be told, the time we spent getting ready to go out and then dissecting the evening later at the diner over bran muffins and decaf was even more fun.

When I moved from Somers to Stonybrook, Long Island, to open the first Nine West store in the Smith Haven Mall, the magic followed me. One night after work, my girlfriend Jackie came over to visit because she was upset about her boyfriend breaking up with her.

"Jackie, you have to have hope," I said, sitting across from her at my kitchen table. "You need to be with somebody who deserves you, not that jerk!"

Jackie looked at me in disbelief, just as Kimby and

Liz had. But I was persistent. I was living in a house share at the time, and I had plans to go to the circus with my housemate, Shane. While he was not my type, Shane—an electrical engineer—was most certainly a catch by most women's standards. Being recently heartbroken, Jackie wasn't exactly in the mood for the circus. I convinced her to come along anyway. I had a hunch she might be glad she did.

Needless to say, I was the maid of honor at Jackie and Shane's wedding.

I would be lying if I said the term "always a bridesmaid, never a bride" didn't cross my mind on occasion. Still, I knew that just because these particular love stories weren't about me didn't mean I wouldn't have a story of my own. I was hopeful for myself when it came to finding the right person, but I wasn't actively on the hunt at that point. I was choosing instead to trust my deep inner sense that there was a bigger plan out there for me. Sometimes I would get discouraged, for sure, but every time I saw these couples connect and witnessed the love between them, I knew that the answer was hope. Love was possible; it was bound to happen. How could it not? It was only a matter of time. (That's how I felt throughout my twenties and thirties, at least.)

That said, I had my limits. Even if I didn't mind my role behind the scenes in the romantic lives of my friends, there were times when playing Cupid could, quite frankly, get a little irritating. When my cousin, Steph, who's four years my senior and the closest thing I have to a sister, invited me to a party in Long Island, I spent much of the evening trying to convince her not to give up on love and that she was a valuable and worthy person, just as I had with Jackie. That part was fine—I didn't mind being a cheerleader. When we were on our way home from the party, though, and she asked me to stop at a pub in Katonah called the Tenth Inning, I wasn't enthusiastic. But Steph said she needed a soda for the drive home, so we stopped.

The bartender was a guy named Eric, and he zeroed right in on Steph. He was in a band called The Dates, he told her. Had she ever heard of it?

Steph played it cool. "Well, I don't have your poster on my wall," she said.

"Where's your boyfriend?" he asked.

"I don't have one," she said. "Where's your girl-friend?"

"I don't have one," he said.

* * *

I spent the rest of the evening avoiding the advances of Eric's roommate, but at least the evening was a success for Steph, which I discovered back at Eric's place when I went to use the bathroom and found her there in a man's bathrobe. I looked her up and down, and in my best Bugs Bunny wiseacre voice, I said, "So, you made it to the bathrobe phase?"

We both doubled over laughing. "The bathrobe phase" was a catchphrase we used for years—long after Steph inevitably married Eric. One more happy couple!

While all these experiences were beautiful and helped to affirm my belief in love and fate, some were more profound than others—like what happened with my friend Sharon Floman.

Just like with my other girlfriends, Sharon and I shared a deep soul connection. I preferred spending time with people one-on-one as opposed to in big groups, so each of my friends held a very special place in my heart. Sharon was Jewish and born in Brooklyn (with the accent to prove it). Like me, Sharon came from a tight-knit family and was a devoted aunt to her nieces and nephews. Though our faiths were different, our values were the same: God, family, and someday (hopefully) marriage. We would sit and chat for hours over bagels and coffee, smoking cigarettes and lamenting the state of our love lives. In her mid-thirties, Sharon was a few years older than I was, and she felt that time was running out. Though she was hilarious and smart and attractive, Sharon had a habit of attracting the wrong kind of guy. But I wasn't about to let her give up. It didn't matter if all these men couldn't see the beauty in Sharon; I did. Just like Sharon saw the beauty in me. I didn't call her Sharon, of course. I called her Flo or sometimes Flois Lane.

So, one summer night, even though it was pouring rain and Flo didn't want to go anywhere, I called her up and informed her that she was coming out with me and our friend Joanne to one of the most happening spots in town—a place called Coco's, an outdoor club right on the water.

"Geri, I really don't feel like it," Flo protested over the phone.

"Sorry, Flois Lane, you don't have a choice," I told

her. "We've been dying to go to this place! You're coming out."

By the time Joanne, Flo, and I arrived at the club, the storm had passed, and the early evening sun was coming through the clouds. The outdoor deck was so packed we could barely make our way to the bar. Despite her initial misgivings, Flo had rallied and was suited up for the occasion. She was the kind of woman who would never go out in sweats with her hair in a ponytail, unless it was just the two of us out on a bagel run. She looked put together even as we squeezed ourselves through the crowd, dodging elbows and tripping over people's feet. Edging closer to the bar, I spotted a guy with curly black hair and bright-blue eyes ordering a drink. He was dressed impeccably, just like Flo. And he was talking on a flip phone, which was still a pretty big deal back then.

"Flo," I whispered under my breath.

"Already saw!" she whispered back.

Immediately, I could feel that electricity in the air again. It was like witnessing the hand of fate coming through the storm clouds. When we got up to the bar, the man with the curly black hair immediately made his way over to Flo. His name was Michael, he said. And could he buy us a drink?

A few minutes later, I excused myself to go to the ladies' room and disappeared back into the throng. I knew from experience where this night was headed: Flo moved in with Michael six months later; they were married within a year. Flo and Michael moved to Florida, and the rest, as they say, is history.

Except Flo and Michael were destined for a different kind of history than the other couples. After they got married and moved away, Flo and I didn't speak as frequently—not because we were any less close, but because our lives were branching off in different directions. Flo was a wife and, before long, a mother to a little girl; I was a working girl whose career was starting to really take off. I didn't worry if I hadn't heard from Flo for a while, though, because I knew she'd found the perfect man for her and was finally where she was supposed to be. It wasn't until after Flo was eight months pregnant with her second child, a son, that I had a sense something was off with my friend. I woke up one morning from a dream with the urgent sense that I needed to get in touch with Flo. I called her and told her I wanted to come down for a visit.

"Now?" she asked. "They just put me on bed rest. My blood pressure is getting too high, and I could end up having complications."

"Oh my God, I have to see you!" I said. "Listen, I'm on my way."

"No, Geri! I'll be fine! Just come down for the baby's bris. It'll be here before you know it."

Eventually (reluctantly) I gave in and agreed to wait until after the baby was born to visit. But I kept her on the phone for a long time after that. We gabbed for hours, updating each other on our lives. The only things missing were the coffee and bagels. Even though probably seven years had gone by since those days, nothing had changed between us. I was still worried when I hung up the phone with Flo, but it had given me some peace to hear her voice. I just wish I'd known it was going to be the last time.

I'll never forget the sound of Michael's voice when I picked up the phone that day, not long after my conversation with Flo. He was hysterical.

"Geri, Flo's dead."

A wave of ice-cold shock ran through my body. How could this be?

It was their daughter's birthday, Michael told me. Both sets of grandparents were there to visit and help out. Flo had a horrible migraine, so she stayed in bed while the grandparents delivered birthday cupcakes to the little girl's school. By the time they got home, she was gone. Flo died of toxemia in her sleep. Tragically, the baby didn't make it.

I booked my flight to Florida and packed my bag as fast as I could. When I got there, I was met with complete devastation. Flo's parents were destroyed. I doubt either one of them could even see straight. Michael was clearly a man in shock, just going through the motions. I stayed at the house so I could take care of all the little things that had to be done, like keeping the kitchen stocked with supplies. There was nothing I could do to dull the ache of the family's unfathomable loss, but I could help to create some sense of stability and alleviate a little bit of the pressure. I could make runs to the grocery store and tidy up after mourners came to sit shiva.

It was in those moments of simple service, washing the dishes and tidying up the house, that I realized how meaningful my presence was at that time. I'd been there to bear witness at the start of Flo and Michael's relationship, so it was only right that I was there for the end. It was like watching both the birth and the burial of a beautiful thing. And while I was heartbroken, I still believed in my soul that their love was meant to be, and that God had brought them together for a reason. I also believed that this wasn't really "the end" for Michael and Flo. I knew that they'd be together again someday, and for all eternity.

The same couldn't be said for my friend Joanne and her husband Stan, unfortunately. (I should add here that I had no hand in bringing those two together!) Joanne worked with me at Nine West, and shortly after she got married, I noticed a change in her. Joanne was stunning, not to mention loving and kind. She was the kind of person who made the people around her feel good. As a recently wed woman, Joanne's glow should have been shining brighter than ever. Instead, the opposite was happening. It was like her spirit was shrinking. Initially, when I asked her if everything was okay, she swore that she was fine. But when I asked her again a few weeks later, I got a very different answer. Standing across from me in the stock room where we were taking inventory of heels and wedges, Joanne turned to me with a serious look on her face.

"Geri," she said. "I think Stan is having an affair."

Most of the time, when a woman says she suspects her husband of having an affair, a friend responds with something along the lines of "Don't be ridiculous; he loves you" or "You're just being paranoid." My response was of a completely different variety.

"Joanne," I said slowly. "I think I know who the

other woman is."

"What?" Joanne's eyes went wide. "How do you know who it is?"

I understood Joanne's disbelief. I hadn't lived in Long Island for very long and didn't know many people, so how could I have guessed the identity of her husband's mistress? But for some reason, I had a hunch.

A young woman had come into the Nine West store at the mall looking for part-time work recently. In a way, she reminded me of Joanne: beautiful and smart. She seemed like someone who was already successful. I wondered why she wanted to sell shoes part time at a mall. I wasn't hiring then, but I told her to fill out an application, and I put it in a folder with the other applications we kept on file.

I didn't tell Joanne about that woman yet, though. Instead, I made a suggestion: "Let's play a little game," I said. "When the private investigator gives you his report, bring it to me. We'll see if I was right."

A couple of weeks later, the investigator completed his report. Back in the stock room, Joanne handed it over to me. I looked at the name on the report and pulled the mystery woman's application out of an envelope.

It was the same name. A chill ran down my spine. Poor Joanne's jaw was on the floor. It was all too real now.

Joanne wanted a divorce, and I didn't blame her. But Stan threw himself into the role of repentant spouse, promising he'd never do anything like that again and showering Joanne with attention and gifts.

Shell-shocked and sad, Joanne agreed to give Stan one more chance.

Her thirtieth birthday was coming up, and Stan was determined to win Joanne's favor back by pulling out all the stops and throwing her an amazing party. Their backyard was packed with guests and gifts and food, and there was even live music, thanks to Joanne's brother-in-law (who just happened to be Billy Joel's sax player). Joanne played along for most of the night, smiling and laughing and making conversation. No one ever would have guessed what she was planning—not even me! But just before she blew out the candles on her cake, Joanne leaned over to me and whispered something I'll never forget: "I'm leaving my husband tonight. And you're my getaway car."

Joanne bent over the cake then, and the candles went dark. Everybody clapped and cheered while I tried to process what my friend had just told me. Clearly, this was something Joanne had been plotting for a while.

I believed that marriage was a holy sacrament. I wasn't encouraging her to file for divorce—I hadn't offered my opinion at all. But it was hard to see how a person could get over that kind of betrayal and learn to trust again. And watching Stan act like a devoted husband all night had turned my stomach. So, I decided in that moment to go along with whatever grand escape she had planned.

Joanne looked perfectly calm, serving cake and laughing. Meanwhile, I was getting a serious case of the butterflies. How were we going to pull this off with so many people around? Somebody would spot us trying to leave, for sure.

Eventually, Joanne excused herself from a conversation and gave me a nod. "Follow me," she said quietly.

Joanne led me into the house and up the stairs to her bedroom. She shut the door behind us and pulled a set of packed suitcases out of the closet.

"That's everything," she said.

"Okay," I replied. "Let's go." We crept down the stairs, stifling nervous giggles, and slipped out of the house. We walked to my car in the dark.

She never went back. Stan begged and pleaded, but Joanne was done. She found a humble little fixer-upper, and I helped her get settled in. We stripped cabinets and waxed the floor, drinking wine and listening to music and venting about men. It wasn't the life she'd imagined for herself, but slowly I saw Joanne's spark coming back. She was remembering who she'd been before Stan and that she could be happy on her own. It was a beautiful thing to see.

One night, after we'd gotten the place into pretty good shape, Joanne invited me over. I was expecting it to be just the two of us, but when I arrived there was a little party in full swing. Joanne had hired a psychic for the evening, and everyone was getting a reading. I understood right away why Joanne hadn't warned me in advance: she knew that as a Catholic, I wasn't entirely sure how I felt about things like clairvoyants and mediums.

"I don't know about this, Joanne," I said. "And I didn't bring any money with me."

"That's fine—I already paid for everybody!" Joanne

said. "Come on, Geri, this guy is really good. And I think you could use something like this right now." She gave me a pointed look.

I knew exactly what she was talking about. At the time, I was sinking into a depression over a guy I was dating named Paul. Something about the relationship just didn't feel right, though I couldn't put my finger on it. I should have ended things right away, but I was so tired of starting over that I kept staying, hoping we could make the relationship better. In the meantime, I was unhappy—so unhappy, I realized, that I was willing to give this psychic a shot.

"Fine, fine," I said, finally. "But I'll go last."

Maybe it would get too late and the psychic would have to leave before my turn came around. I still felt uneasy about the idea. But before long, the bedroom door swung open. A dramatic looking man with very animated facial features walked out and looked me up and down.

"Oh my God," he said. "You're the one I'm here to see. And I'm exhausted! Ugh! Oh well, at least now it all makes sense."

I had no idea what he was talking about (and he was kind of freaking me out, to be honest), but I followed him into the bedroom anyway. What did I have to lose?

The psychic sat me down at Joanne's bedside table and took a seat across from me. His eyes were intense. As he looked at me, it felt like he was taking in not just my physical body but the air and energy around me. Finally, he took a deep breath.

"You have angels everywhere," he said, shaking his

head in wonder. "Let me tell you, you are protected. You have tremendous light around you."

I wanted to believe what he was telling me. Who wouldn't? But he probably said that to everyone, I reasoned.

Suddenly, he banged his fist on the table. "Get rid of him!" he said. "This guy you're with, he's twisted and deceitful. You know this already. Listen to yourself! He takes up far too much time in your head and your heart, and he doesn't deserve any of it."

I was shocked. My relationship with Paul was a tango, hot and tumultuous, but I was in love with him. I nodded silently, not knowing what to say.

Then the psychic tilted his head. His focus seemed to shift. "What do you do for a living?" he asked. "Are you a decorator, by chance?"

I shook my head. I was still managing the Nine West store at the Roosevelt Mall then, and I told him a little bit about my job.

He looked puzzled. "Well, you're definitely going to be decorating something in the near future," he said. "Something big. Big career changes coming, too. I see you moving out of state."

Since I hadn't even been living on Long Island for all that long, I had a hard time believing that last prediction. And even though I had a knack for making my homes look good, I definitely wasn't a designer. But I thanked him anyway, and Joanne and I had a good laugh about the whole thing after all the other guests had gone.

"He thinks I'm some kind of interior designer or

something," I said, kicking off my shoes. (Since it was so late, I'd decided to spend the night.)

"He told me I was going to get married, move to Hawaii, and have three kids!" Joanne said, cracking up. "I mean, come on. What are the odds?"

I agreed. "What a whack job," I said.

Still, I didn't forget what the psychic said. The truth was, I didn't love everything about Long Island. The dating scene was horrible, for one thing, filled with phonies and mobsters and drunks and sleazeballs. Joanne and I were always debating if it was even worth going out. On one hand, we were always hopeful, and we didn't want to sit home alone. On the other hand, we were tired of meeting jerks with no real interest in a relationship. Even worse, it was always the same crew of jerks at the same places. Joanne had been dating a bartender who looked like he belonged in the rock band Journey with his shoulder-grazing hair and tight pants.

Another guy we saw every time we went out was Frank. He wasn't a bad guy like some of the others, but he wasn't someone Joanne or I was remotely interested in dating, either. That didn't stop him from trying, though—and it didn't stop us from giving him a hard time. One time, we each drew a fake tattoo of half of a broken heart on our arms. I wrote *FR* in my heart and Joanne wrote *ANK* in hers.

"Maybe one of these days you'll get your wish, Frank," we told him, winking. On some level, the poor guy probably believed us. One night when we were feeling especially bored and fed up, we took our teasing to the next level and actually called Frank.

"Hey, Frank, it's your lucky night," I said. "Why don't you come pick up me and Joanne and take us out?"

"Are you kidding me?" Frank couldn't believe his ears.

Neither Joanne nor I had any intention of doing anything remotely romantic with Frank, but we knew he'd be happy just to hang out. And we had a good time, too, I have to say—until Frank asked us to continue the evening at his friend's house. Joanne was into the idea because she had grown up in the area and knew Frank's friend from years ago, but as the new kid in town, all I wanted to do was go home and go to bed. The night had started out like a joke, which I was fine with. But now I was ready for my pajamas.

"Come on, Geri. Let's go!" Joanne said.

Once again, a girlfriend was pleading with me to play wing woman.

"I'll drive," she promised. "I'm just so curious. Please?"

I couldn't refuse her. I might not have been in the mood to hunt down a love connection, but I was still proud of Joanne for all the progress she'd made since splitting up with Stan.

"Okay, okay," I said, throwing up my hands. "Maybe Frank's friend will be nice. Who knows?"

He wasn't nice. At least I didn't think so. But Joanne seemed to have a decent enough time, catching up on gossip about old high school friends as I sat on the edge of the couch trying to ignore the love-struck look on Frank's face.

I was so relieved to finally get out of there.

"Okay, so it wasn't the best night ever," Joanne admitted on the car ride home.

I laughed. In the grand scheme of things, another few hours wasted wasn't the end of the world. I should have known, however, that those hours hadn't been wasted at all. A couple of days later, Joanne got a call from her brother, who had gotten a call from a friend of Frank's friend. "This guy is asking for your number," Joanne's brother said. "Do you know a guy named Robert?"

Joanne called me right away. "Geri, oh my God! Robert was my high school sweetheart!"

Frank's friend had called Robert, who was home for a visit, after learning that Joanne was divorced.

"Wow, that's so bizarre," I said.

"Yeah, but you haven't even heard the most bizarre part yet," Joanne said. "Robert is in the army, and you're never going to believe where he's stationed!"

Suddenly, it dawned on me. "Joanne, don't even tell me he lives in Hawaii."

Of course, Robert did live in Hawaii. And before long, so did Joanne. Exactly as the psychic foretold, she married Robert and moved to Hawaii. And we didn't know it then, but they would have exactly three children.

Since the psychic had predicted Joanne's future so accurately, I couldn't help but wonder if he'd been right about me, too.

I see you moving out of state, he had said. I did resign from Nine West and move to Pennsylvania to be marketing director for the Granite Run Mall. Still, plenty of people move for work, I rationalized. The psychic probably said that to everybody.

One of my first big jobs in Pennsylvania was to get the mall ready for Christmas. I had a budget of $200,000 for seasonal décor, and I hired a crew of helpers from a nonprofit that put ex-cons to work. I played disco music and ordered pizza for everyone to make the job feel more festive.

"Keep fluffing those bows, boys!" I called from the top of a ladder, where I was hanging ornaments on a twenty-four-foot-tall tree.

It wasn't until that moment that the next part of the psychic's prediction came back to me: *You're going to be decorating something big.*

He'd been right about Joanne getting married and moving to Hawaii. He'd been right about me moving out of state and decorating something big. Did that mean he was right about the angels around me? Was I really protected and surrounded by light? Maybe that was why my presence always seemed to be a catalyst in bringing my friends together with their true loves. Maybe those angels were guiding the people around me. But if all of that was true, why hadn't the angels found the right person for me? When would it be my turn?

Chapter Eight

I'm Solo

Two years earlier, in 1991, a wedding had set the stage for the relationship advice I got from the psychic. My girlfriend Victoria was getting married in Kent, New York, and she invited me and a guest to the wedding. I called Vickie to let her know I'd be going solo. Kent was not far from Somers, so I decided to get ready for the wedding at my parents' house and stay the night there, too.

It was a horrible, rainy day, and it took me hours to get to my parents' home from my Nine West store in the Roosevelt Mall. I was tired from working retail hours, I was exhausted from the stressful drive, and I still faced a forty-minute drive to the wedding. "I actually don't even feel like going anymore," I said to my mother.

But I pulled myself together and got ready, because you never know who you might meet. I wore a white, ruffled, V-neck blouse with bell sleeves, high-waisted black slacks with a self-tie belt, and open-toed, black, sling-back heels. I liked wearing pants to weddings because I loved to dance, and pants freed me from worrying about ripping my pantyhose.

I arrived late. I'd missed the cocktail hour, and the guests had already been seated for dinner. I was assigned to the table for misfit toys—you know the table, where the bride and groom's "leftover" friends and relatives are seated, and no one knows anyone else. The guy next to me had a crackly, high-pitched Boston accent, and I realized after chatting a bit that his guest was the cab driver who'd brought him to the wedding.

That's when I had the feeling that someone was looking at me from a distance. I raised my head and saw a Tom Selleck-as-Magnum PI look-alike approaching my table.

He wore a black tuxedo with a bowtie and had deep, beautiful dimples. He must the best man, I thought.

He stopped behind me, placed his hands on my shoulders, and said, "Hello. I'm Paul."

I turned my head to look up at him and said, "Oh, hello. I'm solo."

"That's an unusual and beautiful name," he said, glancing at the table card, which read *Geraldine Brown & Guest*. His eyes quickly met mine, and I knew that spark. Hope had arrived. In one split second, my life turned from doom and gloom to bright and exciting.

After some small talk, Paul was beckoned to his table, which was out of my view. Being the best man, Paul had to salute the newlyweds. Soon after, the DJ began to play music, and the bride and groom and their families got up to dance. I can never resist good dance music, and I quickly got up to join them.

I'd always loved dancing. I never got the ballet lessons my parents promised when we moved to Somers, but it didn't matter; I danced in my room. At family weddings, my uncles would grab me and swing me around like Ginger Rogers. Dancing was my favorite way to celebrate career victories, too. When I passed the eight-hour exam for marketing director accreditation after a year of traveling forty-two weeks out of fifty-two and cramming for the exam on weekends, I took myself out dancing in Garden City, New York. It was the best night ever. Strangers felt my freedom and energy. They kept asking me, "Where are your friends?" and I'd point to myself and say, "You're looking at them!" Boy, did God give me guts!

At the wedding that evening, I was dancing with one of Vickie's brothers when Paul cut in and took my hand. He led me to a quiet bar in another room and bought me a drink. We hadn't been talking long when his sister came searching for him. She gave me a sneering look. "Paul, you're wanted inside," she said.

"Peggy, this is Geraldine, a friend of Victoria," Paul said to her. Without responding, she just turned and went back to the ballroom. Paul and I exchanged numbers before he got up to follow her.

Our romance began that day and moved quickly into something that I had hoped for my entire life. There were flowers and romantic dinners, and lots of love was exchanged. A few months passed, and the holidays were approaching. Paul invited me to New York City to meet his work friends from Con Edison for a happy hour, and I couldn't wait to see him. I was anxious to introduce him to my family, and I planned to invite him to our Thanksgiving dinner a few weeks later.

Paul introduced me to all the guys. One of his friends bought us each a drink, and then Paul took my hand. "I have to tell you something," he whispered.

As we moved away, I caught a smirk on the face of the man who'd bought our drinks, and suddenly I sensed that something wasn't right. I trailed Paul through the crowded bar to a more private spot. From the look on his face when he turned to face me, I doubted that we'd be celebrating Thanksgiving together. He probably already had plans.

What he said, though, almost knocked the wind out of me.

"I'm engaged."

All I could do was stare into his eyes. I watched his lips move under that manly mustache, but I couldn't hear the rest of what he said. I thought I'd found a man—a real man—to love with all my heart. I thought this man in front of me was going to be my man forever. I flashed back to feeling his hands light on my shoulders the day we met and telling him my name was Solo. I'd even told my mother when I got home that night that I'd met the man I was going to marry.

I *was* solo that night, but apparently, he wasn't. His fiancée was probably at the wedding too. I wracked my brain but couldn't recall seeing him sitting or dancing with anyone in particular. There must have been clues. How could I have been so oblivious?

With tears in my eyes, I forced myself not to show Paul how devastated I was. "How horrible it must be for this woman who is your fiancée," I said. "How deceitful are *you!*"

I was overwhelmed with guilt that I'd done something wrong. All I wanted, in the deepest part of myself, was to be loved, wholeheartedly and unconditionally, for the God-loving girl that I was. How could this be happening to me when my intentions were so loving?

I had to get out of there. I told Paul never to contact me again. I was shaking as I left the bar. He had broken my heart with those two words, and I was in a state of shock.

Tears were my most intimate friends that winter, and I spent another holiday solo.

* * *

The new year was a few days away, and lo and behold, I was still alive. I wasn't happy, but I'd made it through the holidays. Christmas always made me feel closer to God. His arrival as an infant humbled me, and the Gospel reinforces the true meaning of Christmas as the shepherds, the kings, and Mary and Joseph say yes to their callings with undeniable and unshakable faith. That renewed my belief that God has a plan. As we say, "Thy will be done." I hoped that someday, I would understand what his plan for me was.

Then one night after work, the phone rang. It was Paul.

"Jeremiah," he said, "I'm sorry." He told me how miserable he'd been without me. He said he wanted to spend New Year's Eve with me. He wanted to spend his life with me. He had broken off his engagement.

My first reaction was that I was living a fairy tale. I

was Snow White, and I'd awakened to find my prince before me. Then reality set in. Once a cheater, always a cheater, I thought.

On the other hand, maybe our relationship was meant to be. My brother, Christopher, had broken off an engagement a couple of years earlier and almost immediately met Rosalie, the beautiful woman he eventually married. Besides, I could feel Paul's deep regret for hurting me.

I didn't know why he'd called me Jeremiah—I liked the Three Dog Night song about Jeremiah, the bull frog, who "was a good friend of mine." But I knew Jeremiah was also an Old Testament prophet, and when I read his book in the Bible, I found this:

"For I know the plans I have for you," declares the Lord, "plans to prosper you and not harm you, plans to give you hope and a future." (Jeremiah 29:11)

Was that why Paul had come into my life? Was he in God's plan for me?

We started to see each other again. We planned to celebrate my March 12 birthday early, and so on February 26, I drove to Brooklyn to spend the weekend with him. He was still at work when I arrived, but I had a key and let myself in. Something felt off that afternoon, but I couldn't wait to take a long, hot shower, so I took my overnight bag right into the bedroom.

After my shower, I waited and waited, reading magazines and then cutting out pictures and words and creating a message on the glass top of his coffee table. I covered it with Saran Wrap to preserve it, and then I turned on the TV, and that's when I realized that something certainly *was* wrong. Terrorists had detonated a truck bomb in the parking garage under the north tower of the World Trade Center, and Con Edison crews were grappling with the resulting power outage.

That's where Paul was! I hoped and prayed that he was okay, and soon after that, he called to say he wouldn't be home that night.

I couldn't extend my weekend because I'd just started my new job as director of marketing for the Granite Run Mall in eastern Pennsylvania, so we had to reschedule my birthday celebration. I was just glad that he was okay.

A few weeks later, I drove back to Brooklyn. Once again, something felt off when I arrived at Paul's apartment. Again, he didn't answer the door and I let myself in. This time, I heard the shower running. I was already dressed for dinner, but he seemed to be running late.

When I took my overnight bag into the bedroom, the bed wasn't even made, and I decided to make it for him.

It was a queen-size Ralph Lauren-style country bed, and I circled it, tugging the sheets straight. Then, on one of the pillows, I noticed a hairpin. And when I moved the pillow to tuck in the fitted sheet, I found a long strand of blond hair. I'm not a blonde, and I don't use bobby pins. No. Please, no, I thought. This can't be happening!

My stomach ached, and my heart pounded. I went into the bathroom, where Paul had just stepped out of the shower. He was wrapping a fluffy, white towel around his waist.

"Hello, Jeremiah," he said.

I looked at his big dimples, his big smile, and the droplets of water on his broad chest. How I wanted to love him right then and there. We could have a wonderful birthday celebration, dining and dancing and romancing—if I didn't ask the question. But how could I relax if I didn't clear the air?

I took his hand and led him into the bedroom. "Was anyone here with you before I came over?" I asked.

His face twisted. "What? Are you crazy?"

I hadn't expected anger. He was a caring man. "Paul, please, just tell me the truth. I found this bobby pin and a long blond hair that's obviously not mine. Did you have someone else here? Were you in the shower cleaning yourself of guilt just now?"

Instead of embracing me and reassuring me, he was belligerent. He accused me of being insecure. He kept saying that I was crazy. And I knew deep down that he was lying to me. I can't describe the depth of my hurt. I couldn't fathom how Paul could shut off his conscience and behave that way. I grabbed my bag and drove back to my hotel room in Pennsylvania.

Chapter Nine

The Invisible Man

I was heartbroken. In my head and my heart, Paul was still present, but in reality, he was not and apparently never had been. To distract myself from the painful void in my life, I threw myself into work and into finding my ideal rental: I wanted a place of my own that I could call home—like my first rental in Stonybrook had been. Each day, I'd check the listings in the newspaper, circle the ads for "carriage houses," and make appointments to see them.

My new boss, Kevin, was a Mormon from the Midwest. He was thirty-five and had five children, each a mini version of him—smart and clean-cut with wholesome good looks. He liked my New York style of getting things done. I moved faster, talked faster, and made connections immediately, but my pace sometimes made him nervous. Kevin was nice enough to let me leave work to investigate the rentals.

After many go-sees, I found a listing for a carriage house at a gated home. When I pulled into the driveway, I saw a security system along the fence. The property looked like a mobster hideaway, and the lonely man who lived there looked like a mobster. He told me that his wife was in the hospital, dying of cancer. What the listing called a "carriage house" was an upstairs apartment in the main house. The only outside access was a spiral staircase. I asked how I would get a bed up there, and he shrugged.

Next!

My frustration bubbled out in tears when I called my mom that night. She was a great listener, and she was supportive. Even though she missed me terribly, she never said it. She told me that everything would be fine. God had a plan, and maybe I just needed to open my mind to other possibilities. I listened carefully, but deep down, something told me not to give up on the carriage-house search.

I heeded Mom's advice and looked at some apartment complexes that co-workers recommended, only to become more disappointed each day. Then I saw a listing for a carriage house in Glen Mills, which was a town in the mall's primary market demographic, but it felt as though it was in another country compared with the bustling area around the mall. The ad said, "Professional female preferred."

I met the owners, Mrs. Freiberger and her husband, at the main house, which, they told me, had once been owned by Claude Raines, the actor who played the title role in *The Invisible Man*. They walked me down a pebbled pathway across a pasture-like lawn. To the right was a small stable, and a horse grazed inside a fence beside it. The carriage house came into view when we rounded the stable and looked across a vast field.

Little lights outlined a trail to the quaintest stone

house I'd ever seen. It was actually a spring house, with a natural spring underneath it, where, back in Colonial days, horses would drink. It was as welcoming as a gingerbread house in a fairy tale, and I knew I was home.

I signed the lease the same day. The rent was four hundred dollars a month, and it was a ten-minute commute to my office at the mall. The owners were thrilled when they heard my occupation, anticipating that their three little girls would be safe with me as their new tenant.

The mall renovation was in full throttle, and I attended the construction-development meetings every two weeks. All the responsibility for the grand reopening events, publicity, marketing, and holiday preparation was on my shoulders, along with preparations for the consumer giveaways and a private party. All operations were intertwined with marketing efforts, and at each meeting, Alan, the representative for Equitable Life Assurance Society of the United States, the mall's owner, would say, "All right, Geri. What do you have for me?"

I had a $100,000 budget for the grand reopening and $20,000 was set aside to get a big-name athlete to sign autographs at Modell's, our sporting goods store. Alan wanted Lenny Dykstra, the Philadelphia Phillies' center fielder, and my boss, Kevin, had told me to play by the rules.

But I'd followed Dykstra in the tabloids when he played for the New York Mets, and I didn't like him. He was a great ballplayer, but he was a playboy with a record of driving while intoxicated. I phoned the Phillies' office and got phone numbers for every player on the team roster. I called Dykstra first. His manager told me that Lenny would make an appearance for $20,000, but he would only stay for two hours, regardless of how many fans were still waiting in line.

I worked my way down the list to Curt Schilling, a pitcher. "Tell me about Curt," I said to his manager, Mike.

Mike said Curt didn't get a lot of media attention, but he was a great guy. His wife had just given birth, and they'd named the baby *Gehrig* after Lou Gehrig, the late, great New York Yankee.

"How much?" I asked.

"He'll do three hours for $1,200," Mike said.

I signed him on the spot. Worst case, I figured, we'd have two ballplayers signing autographs at the event.

By the time the next development meeting rolled around, however, it was as though a miracle had taken place. Curt Schilling's pitching had helped to seal the National League Championship, sending the Phillies to the World Series, and he had been named the National League's most valuable player. Overnight, his price for publicity appearances shot up to fifteen thousand dollars.

So, when Alan asked me at the meeting, "So, Geri, did you get me Dykstra?"

I said, "No. I got Schilling for twelve hundred dollars."

My boss was thrilled that I hadn't followed the rules. The Modell's president donated baseball caps and balls for Schilling to sign, and ten thousand people showed up at the grand reopening to see him.

I made it to the big time with that decision. But it wasn't the only time I succeeded by breaking the rules. In the late 1990s, the trend of kicking out teenage "mall rats" struck me as short-sighted. So, I decided to invite young people *in*. Working with the Sam Goody music store in the Broadway Mall in Hicksville on Long Island, my team and I set up concerts in the mall featuring new artists such as Mandy Moore, P!nk, and an all-girl band from Ireland called B*witched. Word spread like wildfire, and thousands of kids—and their parents—turned out for the shows.

Following my gut instinct in instances like those always generated good publicity and customer traffic. But the Curt Schilling decision also enabled me to improve my own position, as well as those of every marketing director in the company.

When the general manager and assistant general manager of the Granite Run Mall got bonuses for making the performance goals that year, but I did not, I went to bat for myself. I went into Kevin's office, counted to ten, and then blurted out, "Kevin, if you took me out of the equation, do you think we would have met our performance goals?"

"No," he said.

"Then, do you think it's fair that I didn't get a bonus?" I asked.

Kevin called the head office, and after that year, marketing directors started getting a piece of the bonus pie. My assertiveness paid off for me when Kevin was later promoted and told GGP headquarters that he would not take the promotion unless I got one too. Eventually, we both became regional vice presidents of multiple properties. Kevin became a VP for management, and I became a VP for marketing.

* * *

As I was settling into my new home in Pennsylvania, work was all consuming. I got along with the Granite Run merchants and my staff, but I missed my family and my friends, and of course, my heart still ached for Paul. His lies about the blond hair hurt so much.

When I'd left New York to take the new job, he'd been supportive and said he was proud of me. I'd seen him a couple of times since then, and even though I was managing fine on my own, I couldn't help fantasizing about what it would be like if Paul moved to Pennsylvania, and we got married and had our own life and family. Each night in my quaint little home, I would hear the bull frogs croak, and in between, I'd listen for a car coming down the gravel lane, imagining Paul would come and surprise me with a ring.

I wished that he hadn't deceived me. But I was still in love with him, even though I'd sensed that he wasn't always fully present when we were together. He could never make it for the full weekend. He would come on Saturday night and leave on Sunday—or maybe Monday at the crack of dawn. I began to think that I should break things off for good and move on.

As the November grand reopening grew closer, I was working late most nights to get everything ready for the big day and for kicking off the holiday season the following week, when Mom called one night. "Grandma isn't doing so well. She had a stroke. She fell in the tub, and Uncle Lou found her." Those words crushed my heart. My loving grandma, Rosaria, all by herself, falling in the tub. It humbled me: I'd been crying about my tumultuous love life. But what did I really have to complain about?

Still, I longed to see Paul. On my way to visit Grandma Rosaria in the hospital, I decided to stop at his apartment. As I parallel parked on the street, I saw a tall, eerily handsome man on the sidewalk outside the door to Paul's apartment building. He looked foreign, somehow, and he was peering at me. I gathered my belongings and got out of the car, and when I looked over again, he was gone. A feeling of dread flashed through me. I couldn't put my finger on it, but I knew that something dark was lurking.

That evening, I listened to that voice inside me, and I broke up with Paul, even though it hurt. It just felt like it was time.

I went to see Grandma Rosaria in the hospital, and she was in a coma. I took her hand and whispered in her ear like she used to do to me when I was a child, visiting her in Yonkers. "Deet, deet, deet," she used to say to me. And now I whispered it to her with all the love in my heart. "Deet, deet, deet," I said softly. "I love you."

At that, her eyes opened wide.

"I know you hear me, Grandma," I told her. "Oh, how much I love you. I will keep you close in my heart forever."

Grandma Rosaria died on November 15, the day before the mall's grand reopening. But the owners were happy with the preparations I'd done, and they sent me off with the sincerest of condolences. The funeral mass for my grandmother was said amid white roses sent by the owners of the mall.

Paul never made it to the funeral or the mass. He was a coward and couldn't show his face to my family after the turmoil he put me through.

It didn't matter, though. I was trying to move on. I'd had a few dates with a lawyer, and though I felt that I was just going through the motions, we had plans to hit some golf balls one afternoon. And that's when Paul appeared on the doorstep of my carriage house, unannounced.

He knocked as I was tying my sneakers. He wanted to get back together.

I told him to leave me alone and not to bother me again. But he refused to leave.

I walked by him and got into my car, telling him to leave me alone. But when I drove off to meet my date, he followed me in his car. I pulled over to the side of the road, my emotions running wild. I was still so attracted to him, but I couldn't trust him. I loved him, but I hated him, too.

When Paul pulled off the road behind me, I was almost hysterical. I needed to go home and call my date to cancel. Even though I told Paul to go away, he followed me home. We ended up making love in my little carriage house.

* * *

A few weeks later, I realized that I had missed my period. I assumed the turmoil and stress had thrown my cycle off, but when I took a pregnancy test just to be certain, I saw the truth.

It was surreal, but Paul showed up again that day. I could not fathom what was happening to me. I thought about the psychic that Joanne had hired a couple of years earlier. He'd told me that I'd be moving out of New York, and I had. He said I'd be decorating something big, and I'd just trimmed a twenty-four-foot Christmas tree at the mall. He had told me to "get rid of" the man I was dating. That man was Paul.

But the deepest part of me wanted to be married to him and have a family. I knew, though, that the desire for that life had to come from both of us. With my heart in my throat, I told him that I was pregnant.

Paul's passive expression did not change. "I'll do whatever you want," he said. Not, I love you and I want to have this baby with you. Not, let's have this baby and get married.

I did not hear what I wanted—and needed—to hear, which was that he wanted to build a life with me. Paul was attentive and caring when we were visiting wineries or shopping for antiques or going to the beach. But then I wouldn't see him for weeks. My friend Joanne's experience with a cheating husband cast a shadow over my relationship with him. Was that Paul's thing, too? I had found that blond hair in his bed. Wasn't that a red flag that I should heed? My mother had always told me that I was too trusting; as a child, I'd talk to anyone. At the age of twenty-eight, would that trusting nature maneuver me into a marriage that would be far worse than being single? How much of what I wanted in a marital relationship should I cede in order to get married?

None of it, I decided. I was waiting for the right person to come along, and Paul wasn't that person. His idea of love clearly was far different than mine—I could not count on him. There was nothing wrong with me for wanting the right partner. There was nothing wrong with me for wanting to build a marriage on trust and start my family in a realm of unconditional love.

I could not have this baby.

Perhaps having made that decision once before made it easier to make it again. And as I had before, I stuffed my guilt and remorse deep down inside, and I blocked it out. Paul drove me to the procedure and drove me home, but I remember few details beyond those. When he left, I was sucked into a crippling whirlpool of sadness and grief that manifested itself physically in back pain. I was in so much pain that a work colleague had to come to my house, help me up off the floor, and take me to the hospital, where a sports psychologist acknowledged my physical pain and helped me to see its psychological roots.

I went to confession, and the priest was compassionate and Christlike in comforting me. "God has already moved on, Geraldine," he said, "and now it's time for you to move on." He told me to pray to the Blessed Mother, and she would give me comfort.

I did pray, and I forgave Paul eventually, but I could

not forgive myself. I despised myself for being so gull-ible as to believe that Paul had wanted a life with me. I wished I could share with my mother the truth of what I'd done. She wanted to see me happily married, and here I was, repeating the biggest mistake of my life and then putting on a mask and pretending that everything was fine.

In our family, a special mother-daughter bond seemed to flow from one generation to the next, just like the conception of marriage that we all hold. Mom could feel me from far away. Shortly after Paul left, I received a comforting card from her, even though she did not know the story behind the breakup. On the front was a lioness with one paw around her cub. On the inside, it said, "I feel the overwhelming need to protect you."

My body held on to the grief and shame, and though I conquered the back pain by learning to rollerblade, I suffered devastating migraines. I was still hopeful that I would find Mr. Right, but a little voice in my head began to whisper that I was unworthy of the sacrament of marriage, and the hole in my soul got bigger.

* * *

It took me six years to fully get over Paul, and then it happened in a flash. I was leaving Aruba at the end of a vacation, and in a tiny airport security station that could hold only about a dozen people, I looked up and to my astonishment, my friend Victoria was standing there. She was with her husband, Gene, who was Paul's brother.

I went over and hugged them both. We exchanged the details of our lives—me still single and Vickie showing off her two beautiful sons. I'd never told Vickie what happened between Paul and me, and I didn't plan to ask about him. But something pushed me to say, "How's Paul?"

"Oh, he's married to Kathy," she said, naming the fiancée whom he'd "left" for me. "And he has a son named Noah."

"That's wonderful," I replied, thinking, *Good for him. He moved on, too.* Then that "something" nudged me again. "Vickie," I asked. "How old is his son?"

"He's six," she said.

A deep shudder went through me. Had Paul been married while we were dating? Was Kathy expecting at the same time I was? Or did he already have a son when I told him that I was pregnant?

Joanne's psychic had been right when he told me that Paul was sick in the head and the heart. I'd been right to end the relationship. And though I was stunned by what Victoria told me, I was grateful for the closure that her news provided.

Chapter Ten

A Simple Twist of Fate

Joe George was right, too, when he told me that I was going to face my destiny in 1996, but there was a twist. As I would soon find out, when destiny seems to present itself, we're given a choice: to accept the future being handed to us on a plate, or to listen to that little voice inside telling us our fate lies somewhere else. And, like Joe George said, having to make that choice was indeed a little scary . . . at first.

Since the day I'd met Joe George in the airport, I'd moved to Pennsylvania and shifted from retail to shopping centers. I had been a shooting star at Nine West, but now I was the new kid in a new biz . . . I was the new kid from New York in a company full of midwesterners. I was director of marketing, and that position brought as many opportunities for socializing as it did for professional advancement.

It was my responsibility to coordinate media buys, which required building relationships with local agencies, newspapers, and radio stations. This meant lots of knocking on doors and rubbing elbows at ribbon cuttings and other events. Those doors tended to have men behind them, and as a young, single woman, I might have had better luck than some at getting those doors to open.

Behind one such door was Ray. I'd first met him in 1994. He was a rep for a local radio station, and he was bald with a goatee and looked like tennis pro Andre Agassi, who was dating the actress Brooke Shields at the time. When Ray and I started dating, people commented that I was "just like Brooke Shields—long, dark hair and eyebrows included!"

I liked Ray because he was funny and smart, and he made a great first impression. He was definitely what my mother called "a good prospect." Even so, I wasn't that into him, for some reason—though he was a lot of fun to be around. He lived with two other professional men in a proverbial "bachelor pad," where something was always happening . . . and that something was often a party. We both loved going to the beach and had a blast taking trips to the New Jersey shore. Spending time with Ray was never boring. Still, it wasn't enough. I wanted and needed a deeper connection. Before long, I allowed our romance to fizzle out. Since we were both so busy, that wasn't very hard. I didn't think I'd see him again, and I was okay with that.

But then, in that fateful year of 1996, Ray and I ran into each other again. I can't even remember how or where. Maybe it was because I was still carrying Joe George's message inside of me, but I wanted to believe that our unexpected reunion was more than just a coincidence. So, I decided to give him another chance.

Just like the first time we dated, Ray and I got along really well. In fact, as the months went by and I started leaving more and more of my belongings at his house, it became clear that we got along even better now. It might have had something to do with the fact that we were both filling voids for each other. In me, I think Ray found the family he always wanted: big, lively, and joined at the hip. I grew up surrounded by cousins and aunts and uncles and grandparents. It seemed there was always some reason for everybody to be getting together—either side of the family; it didn't matter— whether it was a holiday or a birthday or a christening or a wedding or just a sunny Sunday afternoon. There was lots of food, lots of reminiscing and storytelling from the "old days," and most of all, lots of love. We all said "I love you" to each other all the time without even thinking about it. It always took an hour to say our good-byes. It was normal to me, but I know now that I was extremely fortunate to be surrounded by so much affection.

I never heard those all-important words spoken aloud when I visited Ray's family, and that made me sad. It wasn't that Ray and his brother and parents didn't love each other; they did, of course. But there was a lack of affection that made me uneasy. I didn't think Ray or his dad or brother gave his mother the respect that she deserved, for one thing. I wondered, should we ever get married, if he would treat me the same way.

I understood why Ray was drawn to me and my loving family. But I was drawn to him for a different reason. Ray played the role of a committed partner, which is what I'd spent so long searching for. He loved me, and he wanted us to have a future together. After dating too many guys who were afraid of getting tied down, for Ray to take our relationship seriously was a big deal. This was what I wanted, right?

Of course, it was what my family wanted for me, too. There was no denying that. They welcomed Ray into our family like he was another son.

My little brother, Richie, was on everybody's minds when Ray and I went to spend Easter Sunday at my parents' house in Somers that year. He was the baby of the family by seven years, while my older brother, Christopher, and I were just thirteen months apart. Richie had just graduated from college and announced that he was moving to Florida, and my mother (being an Italian mama who wanted her babies close) was heartbroken. Something seemed off about my little brother's decision to make the move, but I couldn't put my finger on what the problem was at the time. It was more of a vibe than anything else, a general sense of foreboding.

I was preoccupied with these thoughts of my brother as I stood in my mother's kitchen with Ray, preparing brunch. I wasn't in the most festive of moods, to be honest, and I definitely wasn't feeling particularly romantic. I was holding a frying pan in one hand and had an apron tied around my waist. So, it took me by surprise when Ray dropped to his knee in front of me and held out a ring.

What was he thinking? I could've hit him on the head with the frying pan. (Maybe I should have!) But instead, I screamed, "What are you doing?"

Ray just looked up at me with a smile on his face. Then came the words I should have been thrilled to hear.

"Geraldine, will you marry me?"

"Now?" I said. That's just what came out of my mouth, the word *now*.

Later, I would call Ray's proposal an entrapment, because that's exactly what it was. I was trapped in my mother's kitchen, my parents within earshot upstairs. Ray knew me. He knew the kind of girl I was: a girl who didn't like to disappoint anyone. Especially not in the middle of Easter Sunday brunch.

So, I said yes.

"Mom and Dad!" I yelled up the stairs. "I'm getting married!"

My heart did not agree. I looked down at the ring on my finger. It was a beautiful ring. He'd made the "right" choice. He proposed in the "right" way. He did exactly what he was supposed to do. So, I did what I was supposed to do, too, and accepted his proposal. But was I doing this for me?

I'd always believed that marriage was a soulful, sacred union that was made of authentic love, not a matter-of-fact decision. It wasn't just affection that you could expect to grow into love over time. It was the committed love of two people that grows stronger the longer they are together as "one." This belief was sacred to me even as a kid. In high school, I remember listening to friends talk about their eventual wedding plans:

"I'm going to get married when I'm twenty-six."

"I'm going to have four kids."

"You'll be in my wedding party," and so on.

Those conversations upset me. "But what about the person?" I asked. "You don't even know who the person you're going to marry is. How do you know you'll get married when you're twenty-six? How do you know you'll have four kids?"

My girlfriends just laughed and went on talking about what their wedding dresses would look like and where they would go on their honeymoons. It seemed so silly to me at the time, but their talk was actually much more powerful than I realized. Whether or not they realized it, my girlfriends were in the process of creating their own stories, which they would go on to live out, more or less. In a way, they got what they wanted: husbands, kids, houses, and honeymoons. The problem was, when they envisioned their futures, they only considered the surface details instead of the truly important part: the compatibility . . . the love.

Let's just say it didn't surprise me much when a couple of those friends went on to get divorced. After I said yes to Ray, I thought about those girls and how their stories turned out. I felt sick to my stomach. Would my story be any different?

As soon as I got engaged, I was trying to figure out how to get out of it, even though I couldn't help but like the way it felt to be somebody's fiancée. Driving down the street with my hand out the window, looking at the way my diamond sparkled in the sun . . . that made me feel good. Like I finally belonged to someone. I just wasn't sure if it was the right someone.

Because I was so conflicted, most of the things I needed to do to plan for my wedding felt like a chore. Shopping for a wedding dress is something women fantasize about for their entire lives, but I hated every

117

single minute of it (even though my girlfriends did their best to make the experience fun). I put off my mother's offers to help, even though I knew she was dying to get involved. Ray's mother was excited about our impending nuptials, too, and was even supportive of his decision to become Catholic. Ray had been raised Lutheran, but the religion had never really resonated with him. Since he'd started going to church with me, on the other hand, he was showing a new interest in faith and spirituality. I hoped that this was because Catholicism truly meant something to him. Secretly, though, I worried that he was converting just to make me happy and to fit in better with my family—especially when he got upset with me for refusing to accompany him to religious education classes.

"What do you mean, you're not going with me?" he asked.

"Of *course* I'm not going with you!" I said, laughing. "I'm already Catholic!"

"Yeah, but I'm doing this for you," he protested.

"I don't want you to do this for me. Don't do this for me," I said. "Do it for *you*. You should become a Catholic because you love the religion. This is your faith, your relationship with God. It has nothing to do with me."

Ray didn't get it. He wanted to get it, though. I knew he wanted to understand what my faith meant to me—he even wanted to pretend he felt the same way. But he didn't, and he couldn't. He was looking for the free ride.

This lack of understanding extended to Ray's idea of family, too. He wanted to be included in a real, loving brood in the same way that he wanted to be part of a religious community. But he wanted these things without really knowing what they were all about or doing the hard, emotional work that came along with both experiences.

One night, I had a horrible dream about my little brother, Richie. I woke up with a sick feeling in my stomach about my brother and a sense of growing panic. Since I was scheduled to head down south for a business meeting the next week anyway, I made the snap decision to visit my brother in Jacksonville, Florida, which wasn't far from where I was headed. That morning, I told Ray about my plans. He did not take the news well.

"What are you talking about?" he asked. "We have tickets to the horse show this weekend!"

The horse show was sponsored by Ray's radio station, so we were expected to make an appearance. As someone who prided herself on her work ethic, I understood that Ray took his professional obligations seriously. But family trumped business, as far as I was concerned. The fact that Ray reacted so childishly and with such anger showed me that this was one area where our core values definitely did not align. "I'm sorry to disappoint you," I said, trying to stay calm. "But I'm going to see my brother."

I left Ray to pout and called my mother.

"I just wanted to let you know that I'm going to go down to visit Richie when I'm on my trip this week," I told her.

My mother immediately started crying. "I had a horrible dream about your brother," she said.

My heart started pounding. I wanted to tell her that I'd had a dream, too, but I didn't. "Don't worry, Mom," I said. "I'll go and check on him. Everything will be fine."

* * *

When I first saw my brother in Jacksonville, it seemed like maybe everything really was fine. Richie looked good, at least. But then, he had always been a hand-some kid. As a little boy, his golden ringlets and big eyes made him look just like an angel. I couldn't have loved him more. But if I'm honest, I also thought he was a little bit of a spoiled brat. Not that it was his fault—as the baby of the family, he'd had more advantages than my older brother and I had; my parents were in a bet-ter place financially when he came along. Plus, because Christopher and I were so much older, we spent more time doting on him than teasing him . . . especially me. I loved taking my brother out and buying him Polo outfits, dressing him like a prince. I was so proud of him, and I just knew he had so much potential.

It was that potential I was afraid was being wasted now. In a way, Richie was living every young guy's dream: he was sharing an apartment right on the ocean with his college roommate and working on a tugboat (but really spending most of his time smoking pot and learning how to surf). Part of him was perfectly content with his chilled-out, beach-bum lifestyle, I could tell. But another part of him was unsatisfied. After all, my career was on an upward trajectory, and Christopher was the director of a hospital. Richie knew, on some level, that he was meant for something bigger. As we sat on the deck, watching the sun set over the water, he slowly started to open up.

"I don't know, Sis. I guess I'm having fun, but I didn't go to school to work on a tugboat," he said.

"Look, Richie, this isn't forever," I told him. "This is your for-now plan, and you chose it. But if you're not happy, you can always come home. Ma misses you like crazy."

Richie was quiet. I could still see that angelic boy with the ringlets when I looked at him, but he had an edge to him that wasn't there before he left for Florida, an air of anxiety—almost paranoia.

"Can you help me with my résumé?" he asked finally.

"Of course, I can help you," I said. "But you have to do the work. If you want to be successful, you're going to have to make it happen on your own."

At that point, in the back of my mind, I was still thinking that Richie's troubles had to do with his being spoiled and maybe even a little lazy. I was trying to take a "tough love" kind of approach, not wanting to enable him any more than I felt my parents had unwittingly done. But something didn't feel right.

The next afternoon, I went to the water alone to think. It was an overcast day, so I had the beach mostly to myself. Everything was quiet except for the sound of the waves and the occasional sea gull's call. I spread my blanket out on the sand and sat down. I should have been concentrating on work—the main reason for my trip to Florida—but I was so disturbed by the feeling I got from my brother that I couldn't focus. Instead, I lifted my eyes to the gray sky and prayed for a sign that he would be okay. Tears poured down my cheeks.

Please, show me how to help him.

At that moment, a white dove flew over and landed on the edge of my blanket. As it sat, fluttering its wings, I noticed that it had a black mark on its chest. I found its presence comforting, as doves symbolize the Holy Spirit. I took a deep breath. God was listening.

Later that night, after Richie got home from working on the tugboat, we sat on his deck talking. Suddenly, a dove flew over and sat on the railing. I looked at the bird and saw a black mark on its chest. It had to be the same bird that landed on my blanket that afternoon!

"Oh my God, Richie," I said. "This same dove came and sat on my blanket when I was at the beach today, and that was a couple of miles away!"

Richie raised his eyebrows. "That's freaky," he said.

"It's a sign!" I said, excited. "This is the Holy Spirit talking to you, Richie. You should go back to church. Pentecost Sunday is coming up—that's the feast of the Holy Spirit!"

"I don't know about all that," Richie said, shaking his head.

"You need to do something to get centered," I told him. "You need something more than this life. Admitting that doesn't make you a failure. Having the strength to realize you're in the wrong place makes you more of a man, not less of a man. You're more of a man if you leave the wrong situation than you would be if you stayed and stuck it out because of your pride."

Unfortunately, it didn't seem like Richie wanted my advice. What he did want was money, but I refused to give him any. It wasn't that I didn't feel he deserved my generosity; it was that I knew somehow that money wasn't what he needed. Richie was headed down a dark path, and a loan wasn't going to stop him. I was afraid nothing would.

I left the next day, still feeling uneasy. As I unpacked my bags, I tried to tell my fiancé about my fears.

"This is serious," I said. "Something really not good is happening down there."

"He'll be fine," said Ray. "You worry too much. He's just being a beach bum. He'll pull it together."

But once again, my intuition was on target. A week after I got home, my brother Christopher got a call: Richie had an altercation on the beach with several police officers and got the beating of his life. To this day, I don't know exactly what happened. But my father drove down to Florida immediately to pick Richie up, and Christopher and I both headed home from Maine and Pennsylvania, respectively, to my parents' house in Westchester so we could deal with the problem as a family.

"You're really leaving again?" Ray asked as I re-packed my bags.

"This is my little brother," I said. "What do you want me to do?"

Once I got to my parents' house and my family and I took a hard look at how Richie was doing, it became clear that he needed serious medical attention.

Unfortunately, that kind of care doesn't come cheaply—and medical benefits weren't included in Richie's tugboat gig. My parents were comfortable enough, with my father having worked hard and saved all his life, but they weren't wealthy. I could see how torn up my parents were about how they were going to pay for Richie's treatment. That's when I remembered the $10,000 my mother had given me to put toward my wedding.

"Mom, Dad, listen to me," I said. "I don't need a big, fancy wedding. And I make a good living on my own. I want you to take that $10,000 back and use it to take care of your son."

My parents protested at first, but I could see the relief on their faces. And I didn't hesitate for a second before I made the offer. A wedding was just a party; this was my brother's life we were talking about.

My fiancé didn't quite see the situation the same way. In fact, when I got home to Pennsylvania and told him that I'd given the money back, he went ballistic.

"What were you thinking?" Ray shouted at me. "You're such a bleeding heart! You always give everything away!"

He flew off the handle when I suggested any form of helping my brother that inconvenienced us in any way. His reaction disappointed me beyond belief. I was so shocked by his selfish behavior that I didn't know what to do. How could I spend the rest of my life with someone who didn't appreciate the way I felt about my family? Looking back, I see now that if Ray's heart and mind had been in the right place, he would have valued and admired the generosity I showed toward my brother. He would have respected my dedication. He didn't, and that hurt me. But I still wanted to believe that we could make our relationship work. I wasn't ready to let go of the idea that I had found my destiny at last.

In the end, my brother was fine. He was indeed going through a hard time personally, which my mother and I picked up on, but he worked hard and got through it with God's grace. And I probably would have gone ahead and married Ray if it weren't for a man named Billy Gooch . . . or, as hundreds of children knew him, Santa Claus.

* * *

As anybody who's ever strolled through a mall during the holiday season knows, Santa Claus is big business. When I was director of marketing at Granite Run Mall, most big shopping malls did the same thing every Christmas: they set up a guy wearing a red suit and an obviously fake white beard in a big chair surrounded by winter wonderland-type decorations and charged parents a fee for letting their kids to climb up on old Saint Nick's lap and pose for a Polaroid. It was a model that had worked for years, so most malls didn't deviate from the formula (the old "if it ain't broke, don't fix it" mentality).

But I've never been one to settle for the status quo. So, when Santa became my responsibility, I was determined to make the most of it. The retail industry looked at Santa photos as more of a service than an actual way to bring in money, but I saw the whole thing as a huge opportunity for revenue development. If you're going to do something, why not do it right and make some real cash in the process?

The first thing I wanted our mall to do differently was to stop using Polaroids and convert to digital cameras. All the other malls were still using instant cameras. I knew it would give us an edge to be the first ones to print out digital photos for our customers—plus, we'd save money on film. I took the initiative and found a digital photographer, even though everybody else thought I was crazy.

The second change I wanted to make, however, had to do with Santa himself. Growing up, I loved watching *Miracle on 34th Street*, particularly the scene when Natalie Wood tugged on Edmund Glenn's beard. It seemed to me that an authentic beard was the mark of a true Santa. And there were certainly enough men with facial hair in the world. Why did malls always settle for clean-shaven guys with fake beards that could easily be pulled off by curious toddlers?

Finding the perfect, magical Kris Kringle wasn't going to be easy, of course. Luckily, General Growth Properties gave me the option to hire outside help, even though that was a much more expensive way to go than doing everything in house. So, in a defiant reworking of the marketing plan, I crunched the numbers and hired a consultant named Mark Hanson from Minnesota. He would run the whole Santa show for us in return for a percentage of the photo sales. Now, typically, those sales weren't stratospherically high, but I was taking a chance that my new approach would break records.

When I first spoke to Mark Hanson on the phone, I was surprised to feel a little spark between us. Not only was I engaged, but I'd never even seen the guy's face! Still, I wanted to meet him. He was planning to fly to Pennsylvania and offered to take me out to dinner. I couldn't help feeling a little flutter of excitement about our upcoming dinner, even though it wasn't really a date. It was just business, I told myself.

In the meantime, I focused on finding Santa. And Mark had the perfect candidate: Billy Gooch of Cold Spring, Colorado. Billy Gooch looked exactly like the Santa that every child dreams about: fluffy white beard, twinkling eyes, rosy cheeks. Any kid who sat on Billy Gooch's lap would think he was giving his Christmas list to the real deal.

Billy Gooch was also expensive—very expensive. He was going to cost us $30,000, but he would work for the entire season. I decided he would be worth it, but I was going to make the most of every penny we spent. I flew out to Minnesota to meet with our ad agency and brainstorm about the best way to let the world know our mall had the best Santa in the biz.

The ad people agreed Billy was "beautiful." Once I had the team on board, my instructions for them were simple. "Tell my customers this guy wants to see them," I said, pointing to Billy's head shot. By the time I got home, a fax had come through proving that my advice had been taken very literally. The concept was simple but brilliant: Billy as Santa Claus with the words "This guy wants to see *you*." It was perfect.

It also turned out to be very effective, thanks to the full-on marketing blitz my Granite Run team and I orchestrated. We made sure that gorgeous bearded face was everywhere: on the backs of buses, on direct mailers, on buttons. Local radio stations and newscasters, hungry for holiday human interest stories, couldn't get enough of Billy Gooch. Before long, the buzz had gotten so out of control that Santa Claus impersonators from all over the tri-state area were coming to see our Kris Kringle for themselves!

My original goal had been to make my company $40,000 in Santa photo sales, and it was a goal I really needed to reach, considering that I'd gone considerably over budget on the project. But we didn't make $40,000. We made $110,000. Flabbergasted, upper management flew me right back to corporate headquarters to interrogate me. They had countless questions about how we managed to pull off the biggest boon in Santa photo sales they'd ever seen, but they all boiled down to one: "How did you do this?"

My answer was simple: "I treated Santa like a business instead of a service." And it was the truth. To me, the approach was an obvious one, an example of good business sense, not to mention good common sense. But because I was the first one to trust my gut and take the risk, I made a huge impression on my bosses and earned myself the reputation of an innovative self-starter. Though I didn't fully realize it at the time, this was another major sign that even in business, my instincts were usually on target . . . and that something bigger than myself was guiding me in the right direction.

So, Billy Gooch changed the course of my career, but he also changed the course of my personal life. No, I didn't leave my fiancé to run off with Santa Claus. But the man who brought me to Billy Gooch in the first place did set the thoughts in motion that would lead me to break off my engagement to Ray.

When Mark Hanson and I finally met for dinner in Pennsylvania, I had that same flutter of nerves and excitement in my stomach that I'd felt when we spoke on the phone, but I was still telling myself that this feeling was ridiculous. I was engaged to Ray, and that was that. Or was it? Looking into Mark's crystal-blue eyes over my menu at dinner, I was less sure than I'd ever been. What am I doing, marrying this other guy? If Ray were really the one, would I be feeling this way about a man I barely knew?

Somehow, Mark must have picked up on what I was thinking. After some casual banter and business talk, he nodded his head in the direction of the diamond on my finger. "I see you're wearing a ring," he said. "Tell me about your wedding plans."

Any other bride would have lit up at a question like this one, but I felt as though a shadow had suddenly descended upon our table. "It's just another event to organize," I said, shrugging. "I do this for a living. It's no big deal."

Mark gave me a look. "Geri, I don't know you that well," he said, clearing his throat. "So, I'm only going to say one thing: be honest with yourself."

Mark's words hit me with the force of a freight train. I *wasn't* being honest with myself. I was marrying Ray for the wrong reasons, listening to my head instead of my heart. But why? This wasn't like me. I wasn't somebody who compromised my beliefs just to fit into some kind of mold or meet someone else's expectations. Mark was practically a stranger, and already he seemed to understand that much about me. But my own fiancé was clueless. I knew in that moment that I could not go home and look Ray in the face as if nothing had ever happened. I knew without question that I had to break up with Ray that very night.

And that's exactly what I did. It was a turning point: I was following my gut about love, even though doing so set me back to square one. I won't lie; ending my engagement to Ray was sad. Our lives were so intertwined that splitting up meant losses on both sides. It meant the death of a dream, a dream that we had shared with each other and with our friends and family. The process of breaking up wasn't going to be easy, and I dreaded all the little painful details that would soon follow—the conversations, the divvying up of belongings. But more than anything else, I felt relief. Relief that I wouldn't have to lie to myself or anyone else anymore. Relief that I was again allowing myself to listen to the inner voice that had always guided me. Most of all, I was relieved that I had the courage to get to the truth of the matter and follow my heart.

Looking back, I see that Joe George was right: I had met my destiny in 1996. I was destined to succeed in business by following my gut instincts, and I broke off an engagement to the wrong guy. I was managing both of my goals—the one represented by the businesswoman in the pencil skirt on that magazine cover I'd seen years earlier and the one I'd grown up with of finding a man who understood love the same way I did. I wasn't a rookie in either pursuit anymore. I just wasn't sure where I was headed next.

Chapter Eleven

The Power of Nineteen

After going through the huge trauma with my brother and splitting up with Ray, things about my life stopped making sense. I wasn't able to just fall in line anymore. A deep resistance was brewing inside me, and it was beginning to come out in ways I sometimes couldn't predict or control.

One such incident took place at a corporate conference, which just happened to begin on my birthday. The keynote speaker was Gordon Mackenzie, a former designer and writer for Hallmark Cards who had published an award-winning book called *Orbiting the Giant Hairball: A Corporate Fool's Guide to Surviving with Grace*. He was going to give a talk on creativity and innovation. All the bigwigs from our company would be there, including the CEO and the president. They were hoping the presentation would inspire us to think outside the box and take some risks. But the impact it had on me wasn't what they were expecting.

Gordon had a fascinating approach, and I was actually immersed in his presentation. He had nineteen pieces of paper with him, which he hung on a clothesline across the stage. Each piece of paper represented a story and a corresponding lesson. He asked the audience to call out different numbers; based on the number called, he'd choose what story to tell. If anyone called out the number nineteen, however, he said the presentation would end. He didn't explain why.

I was taking notes like a locomotive. I don't even remember writing them, but when I look back at them now, they make perfect sense. Still, I was feeling more and more restless. About an hour and a half into the presentation, Gordon asked the audience for another number. We probably had about another forty-five minutes to go, so there was plenty of time for several more stories. Suddenly, something came over me. Before I could stop myself, I screamed out "Nineteen!" I said it so loudly that I was afraid the woman sitting next to me would have a heart attack.

The entire room went dead silent.

"Thank you very much, ladies and gentlemen," Gordon said, and jumped off stage.

The deafening silence lasted for another couple of seconds. Then Gordon jumped up on the stage again. "The person who called out 'nineteen,' can you please stand up."

I felt all the blood rush to my head. Slowly, I rose from my seat. I could feel hundreds of eyes on me.

"Can you please give everyone here your name and phone number, so they can contact you and ask you why you did what you did?"

I obliged. "Geri Brown," I said. "My number is 516 . . ." I felt like I was having an out-of-body experience or watching myself speak on a movie screen. Part of me felt like I should apologize, but I wasn't sorry. Yes, people were enjoying the presentation, and maybe learning from it. But every story Gordon told was about a game-changing disruption that shifted the way people had been thinking. I didn't believe for a second that his talk would make a difference in the way our company operated, because most of the people listening weren't ready to be disrupted—or disruptive. For the betterment of the company, something had to give, and I was willing to take that chance.

From the other side of the room, Mary Kiley, a senior VP of marketing, waved me over.

I'm done, I thought. My legs were shaking. I walked over to Mary in a daze. People kept calling out to me: "Geri, why did you do that?" One senior executive even accused me of wrecking the whole conference. I just kept thinking, *You don't get it.*

Mary put her arm around me. "Are you okay?" she asked.

"Not really," I said. "I know you guys spent a lot of money on this speaker."

"It's okay, Geri, really," Mary said. Much to my disbelief, she led me over to Gordon Mackenzie.

"Gordon, I want you to meet Geri Brown," she said.

I expected Gordon to be angry, but he was totally cool. He smiled and shook my hand. "Nice to meet you, Geri," he said.

"It's a pleasure to meet you," I said.

"Gordon, I'm curious," Mary interrupted. "Has this ever happened before?"

"Once in ten years," Gordon said, nodding.

"What happened?" I asked, tentatively.

"The person had an epiphany," Gordon said, looking into my eyes. "Is that what happened to you?"

I couldn't speak. I was freaking out on the inside, but I nodded. I certainly had: nothing changes unless something or someone disrupts the status quo.

Gordon didn't look surprised. He pulled out a book and signed it.

"Stay out of the hairball," he said, handing me the book.

* * *

I went back to my hotel room and pulled out my journal, then I broke down in tears. I kept thinking about my brother and the overwhelming love I had for him. He needed to understand that it was going to take courage to change his life, the same kind of courage that it took for me to call out the number nineteen. That courage wasn't just going to show up. He would have to dig down deep for it. It was like he thought he was entitled to courage, just like the people in the room that night felt entitled to be entertained. I was so frustrated—and so tired of being frustrated.

My phone rang.

"Oh my God, girl, what did you do?" It was my girlfriend and coworker, Angie. "Everybody's talking about you! What were you thinking? Oh, and happy birthday!"

"Honestly, Angie, I don't think I'm going to go to the dinner tonight." I was supposed to be heading to a big, fancy reception that night along with all the other major players in my company, but I didn't feel like I could face all those people and their questions. Especially since I had probably just harpooned my job.

"You just stop that right now," Angie said. "You're different from everybody else, and that's a good thing. Just be that Geri Brown you know is in there and don't give it a second thought."

That little vote of confidence was all I really needed to get into gear. I wrote in my journal to clear my head, got dressed for dinner, and headed out the door. I was a little late—even though I'd made the decision to be bold, I was still afraid inside. When I walked into the ballroom, it was like the parting of the seas. Everybody stopped and looked at me. Mary rescued me from the awkward pause by motioning me to me to sit with her, our CEO, Gordon Mackenzie, and our president, Bob Michaels. They all looked surprisingly happy to see me. I started to relax, just a tiny bit.

That's when some brave soul approached Gordon and pointed to me, almost as if I wasn't an actual human being with eyes and ears. "So, has this ever happened before?" the man asked.

Gordon repeated his answer from earlier, telling him once in ten years.

"Why do you think she did that?" the man pressed, still talking about me like I wasn't there.

Gordon gave me an amused look. "Well, she had an epiphany!" he said. "Why don't you ask her about it?"

But the man just looked at me nervously and walked away. Like many of the other people there, he didn't know what to say to me or how to react. Others were obviously on my side, giving me the thumbs up from across the room or winking at me. Some even thanked me, telling me I'd changed the tone of the conference for the better. Still others seemed angry or upset about what I'd done. Another group of people thought I'd been a plant, and that the whole thing was part of the show. In fact, the people who were closest to me assumed this to be the case; my immediate supervisor all but disowned me, he was so embarrassed by the role he thought I'd played.

All the attention made me want to retreat into myself. After being the catalyst for so much controversy, I found myself naturally switching into observer mode. I watched the ripple effect of my actions play out in the words and gestures of everyone in the room and realized that what happened was no accident.

The next day was the last day of the convention, when a panel of senior executives hosted a question-and-answer session moderated by Mary Kiley. This was the first year our company was hosting this kind of panel, part of its efforts to be more transparent and forward thinking. Twenty years earlier, senior execs would never have made themselves accessible in such a way. But on this night, they sat and gamely answered questions about whether we were going international and which companies we were and weren't acquiring. Toward the end of the evening, Mary announced that there was only time for one more question, and she'd be answering it. A woman stepped up to the mic. Her question caught me completely off guard.

"I want to know, was Geri Brown a plant?" the woman asked.

A rustle went through the crowd, but Mary handled it like a pro. "If you had a problem with what Geri did, why didn't you stand up and say something at the time?" Mary asked the woman. "If you disagreed with what she said, why didn't you counter her?"

The woman sat back down without answering. I let out a sigh of relief.

That night was our awards ceremony, and the seating arrangement wasn't revealed until the end of the day. I scanned the names on the list and saw that I was placed right next to the CEO and the president. Everyone started joking around about adding a "noser" to the end of my name, which I had to laugh about. What I'd done to get seated with the president was the opposite of brownnosing!

When I took my seat, Bob Michaels, the president of the company, leaned over. "Geri Brown," he said, shaking his head and smiling.

"Bob, I have my resignation letter written in my head," I said.

Bob laughed. "Are you kidding? Resignation? No. I have just three words for you," he said. "You're my hero."

Chapter Twelve

Emma Jean & Frog

I've always said that I'm a kid at heart, and no one who knows me has ever argued with that. One of the signs of my childlike nature is my willingness to see meaning and wonder in everyday things that most adults are too distracted and cynical to pick up on. Another is my love for things that are maybe a little bit silly, like teddy bears and stuffed frogs.

In fact, frogs and teddy bears (or one teddy bear, anyway) have very special meanings for me. I've always been fond of frogs. I even kissed the ones my brothers and I used to catch—though I never kissed the one that lived in the basement of my little stone house in Glen Mills.

Back in Colonial times, that building had been a spring house, and the spring it was built over still existed in the basement, where my washer and dryer were located. A bullfrog lived there, and he would come out of the spring and sit on the cement floor, watching me as I did my laundry. If I turned up the music, he would croak loudly, and if I turned it off, he'd stop. I told people that I had a singing frog, but no one believed me, because if anyone went down to the basement with me, the frog would jump into the spring and disappear. It became a running joke with my parents, who always asked, "Did you get to kiss the frog yet?"

But my fixation with the amphibians didn't come into focus until years later, when my older brother, Christopher, was living in Bar Harbor, Maine, with his wife and three daughters. As their only blood aunt, I have a unique bond with my nieces (Molly, Ruby, and Bella Brown). I didn't get to see them all that often, because Bar Harbor was quite a trek from my home base. Fortunately, my jet-setting corporate life occasionally took me to places like Buffalo, New York, that were just a short flight away, so I at least saw them about four times a year. This was enough for them to know me as someone who loved them and would always be there for them, and for people around town to know me as "Aunt Geraldine."

Of course, everybody in town already knew the Brown girls. They were three beautiful little kids with big personalities. I could see myself in them. I treasured the time I was able to spend with them, but one trip stands out in my memory as even more special than the others. Molly, Ruby, and Bella were nine, five, and four years old, respectively. My brother and sister-in-law were busy at work, and I had the opportunity to act as a stand-in parent. I oversaw all the daily activities: picking them up at daycare, taking them to the YMCA, taking them out for chicken fingers and French fries. I loved every second of it.

One afternoon, I took them to the park overlooking Bar Harbor's coastline, an emerald-green field on a rocky cliff, surrounded by majestic pines. The girls looked out at the whale-watching area and rolled down the hill, laughing uncontrollably. I kicked off my shoes and rolled right down with them. The sky was picture perfect, clear and blue with just a few puffy white clouds, and the temperature was just about seventy degrees. I was getting dizzy from all the tumbling, so I stood up, and looking up at that perfect sky, I said a prayer of thanks. I was so overwhelmed with all the joy I had inside me that a huge lump was forming in my throat. I had to hide my face, or my nieces would have thought something was wrong.

When I looked down, I noticed a man sitting nearby. He was in front of me, but far enough away that I could only see his back. He was sitting in between two young boys, and they were spending the afternoon the same way I was, it seemed. I wondered if he was the boys' father or an uncle or some other friend or relative. Strangers who saw me with my nieces often assumed that I was their mother, which might have made another single woman in my position feel sad, or at least wistful. But I didn't. All I felt was pure joy and gratitude for the time I could spend with the girls. For some reason, I guessed that the man with the two boys might be feeling the same way. So, I took a picture of the three of them, just to have a reminder of that deeply reflective moment.

When I got home, I plugged the chip from my camera into my computer to download and edit the photos. As soon as I saw the shots from that afternoon pop up on my screen, it was like I was rolling down the hill at the park again. The blue sky, the green grass, my nieces' sweet, smiling faces. Then, I got to the picture of the man and the two boys. Something told me to zoom in on the man, who had something written on the back of his T-shirt. As the letters came into focus, my jaw dropped. His shirt read: "F.R.O.G.," and then, in parentheses underneath, "Fully Rely on God."

That was it for me. From that day forward, frogs were no longer just cute little creatures. They were a symbol of a moment when I'd felt completely and totally immersed in the family and beauty around me. I started collecting frogs, and frogs started finding their way to me, too. I traveled to Florida for a strategic-planning meeting with a general manager, and when I told her about the man with the F.R.O.G. shirt, she was visibly moved. I arrived back home to find a box waiting for me. A giant stuffed bullfrog was inside. Made of leather with big glass eyeballs, he had something of a sinister look to him. Whenever I had a new visitor, it always seemed like the frog's eyes followed him around the room. I decided that frogs were a symbol of God's protection, and even though it sounds crazy, I always felt safe with my new frog around.

As a catechism teacher, I found frogs to be an incredibly useful tool. I opened my first class with the story about the man at the park in Maine, and I brought the photo and my big bullfrog along as props. I showed my third graders the picture and asked them, "What do you suppose this man is thinking about?"

"He's happy to be with his kids," said one child.

"He's thinking, 'What a beautiful day,'" said another.

"He's thinking about how good God is," a third child answered.

Then I showed them a close-up of the man's shirt. The whole class gasped.

"Wow!"

"That's cool!"

"No way!"

I brought along a roll of frog stickers, too, which I would hand out as prizes when kids got the right answers. One day, a girl asked me if she could have an extra frog sticker for her little sister. It was the kind of request I would have made as a kid, so naturally, I said yes.

A couple of days later, I got a call from the director of the program, a very stern woman named Irene. I had a lot of respect for Irene, who did wonderful work and had even started a program for autistic children to make their sacraments. But she was very old school and very strict. And right now, she sounded concerned. She had spotted a frog sticker on the hand of one of our younger students, she told me, and when she asked the little girl where it came from, she got a rather perplexing answer.

"It came from Miss Brown!" the little girl said. "Don't you know that God is a frog?"

Irene cleared her throat. "I'm not sure what you're teaching these kids, Geri, but—"

I cracked up laughing. The little girl was, of course, my student's younger sister, and she clearly hadn't fully understood her sibling's retelling of my frog story. Once Irene heard my explanation, she was able to see the humor in it, thankfully.

The next year, when I told my class the frog story, I added the part about the little girl. They thought it was hilarious, because they were now "big" kids. Since the previous year, the Catholic school at the church where I taught had been closed, but the building hadn't been repurposed yet. So, we moved our program permanently to the school, teaching in empty classrooms that were still decorated and not entirely cleaned out.

After I told them about F.R.O.G., one boy raised his hand to tell me that his pencil point had broken. I hadn't brought any extra pencils with me, but I was pretty sure there'd be some in the supply closet at the back of the classroom. I pulled back the curtain, and the first thing I saw was a roll of stickers decorated with frogs that read "Fully Rely on God" and "Forever Rely on God."

The kids screamed!

"Miss Brown, it's like magic!" said one girl.

"This is better than magic," I told the kids. "This is God's way of speaking to us. If you open your heart, God will always show you he's there."

When I told my mother what happened, she looked at me like I had twelve heads. "Geraldine," she said. "You're getting to be too much with this kind of thing."

My mother and I both have tremendous faith, but that comment illuminates the difference between us: she's more reality based, while I have always been comfortable going to the mystical level. I see blessings in everyday minutia. That's just the way I live my life.

Another symbol I used to demonstrate God's

presence to my catechism class was the penny, because of the famous phrase it bears: In God We Trust. For as long as I can remember, I've always been one of those people who finds money everywhere I go. I call it "angel money." While I was teaching, I would bring in all my found pennies and put them in a big frog-shaped bank at the front of the classroom. Then, at the end of the year, each kid got to pick a penny from the bank and write a prayer to go with it. I told them to keep the penny prayers by their beds as a reminder to trust in God.

When I started a new class, the kids invariably called me Mrs. Brown, and I'd say, "That's not me. That's my mother's name and my grandmother's name. I'm *Miss* Brown." I'd explain the difference between *Mrs.* and *Ms.* and *Miss*. But the kids couldn't comprehend that I didn't have children of my own because I seemed so motherly to them. In truth, I never thought I *wouldn't* be a mom. I thought I had my whole life ahead of me to have the family I grew up wanting. I didn't choose my career over motherhood; my career kept me going while I looked for the man who wanted to share the kind of marriage I envisioned.

The kids in my classes carried me through some lonely times. They—and their parents—wrote lovely notes in Christmas cards, and they showered me with holiday gifts, just as they would their moms. One such gift gave me the message I needed at exactly the right moment. It was a granite block with three holes carved into the top for votive candles. Carved on the back were these words: *God has a purpose for you that is held in*

His heart. God has a path for you that is paved with His grace.

I didn't know what my purpose was then, and it was many years before I saw it clearly. But knowing that God had a path for me was as comforting and reassuring as the deepest kind of motherly love.

* * *

I was living in Scarsdale, New York, when my next totem animal came into my life. Things were going well at work, and I was finally starting to feel comfortable spending the money I earned on nice things for myself. I wasn't a huge shopper the way some women are, probably in part because I associated malls with work. But now that I had some extra money to play with, I started getting into brand names. It was more the quality than the status of high-end products that attracted me, but looking back, so many of the things I bought were ultimately frivolous purchases. I bought a pair of Versace sunglasses without giving much thought to the exorbitant price, knowing they were worth the price tag and that they'd last a lifetime. And then I lost them, traveling from one work event to another. I was upset, and I must have sounded so pretentious, babbling to my friends about losing my Versace sunglasses. I didn't realize that at the time, though. I just bought myself another pair of Versace sunglasses, figuring, "What the heck? I can afford them." Within two weeks, I'd lost them again.

When I realized they were gone, I was in my

building's garage. It was dark and dingy, with visible fireproofing on the ceiling and a cement floor. There I was, in my car on my hands and knees, searching under the seats and in between the cushions, cursing at the top of my lungs. I didn't think anyone else was there. I was so crazed I didn't even recognize myself.

Then I turned my head and saw a beautiful teddy bear sitting on the garbage can near my car. She was wearing a little dress with puffy sleeves and a petticoat, like something out of *Little House on the Prairie*. She had a matching bow in her hair. Right next to the garbage can was the doorway to the lobby and one of the stairwells going up to my floor. Suddenly, I realized that my neighbor, a beautiful, older Indian woman, was standing right there. She must have heard everything I said. I was so humiliated. This woman knew me as her quiet, friendly neighbor, and here I was putting truck drivers to shame with the obscenities spewing from my mouth.

"I'm so sorry," I said. "I'm so sorry you had to hear that. I lost something and . . . I guess I just snapped."

My neighbor was speechless. She turned and went inside without saying anything. Now it was just the mysterious teddy bear and me in the garage. I went over and picked her up, and suddenly I felt very grateful. I loved that bear for witnessing a side of me I never wanted to see again. This bear was more precious than a pair of stupid sunglasses.

"You look like an Emma Jean to me," I said aloud.

I took her into my apartment, where she became a permanent resident. Whenever dates came over to pick me up, I introduced her, and I didn't mind it when they looked at me like I'd finally lost it for real. Every time I felt like I was getting a little too big for my britches or started putting too much stock in material things, I looked to Emma Jean as a reminder to stay humble. To this day, Emma Jean and F.R.O.G. sit on my desk. Just having them around helps me to stay focused on the things that really matter to me. And they remind me to always remain open to signs and symbols from above.

Chapter Thirteen

An Evil Curveball

One thing I truly loved about General Growth Properties was my company's dedication to people. The company spent generous amounts of money on leadership-development programs and management excursions in places like Las Vegas. I got my master's degree in shopping-center marketing just through participating in that organization. General Growth Properties really was built on that sort of midwestern mentality of doing right by people, which is why it was so devastating to all of us when the company started struggling.

We were on the verge of the stock market crash of 2008 and one of the largest real-estate bankruptcies in history. Companies of every kind were preparing to file. The tension was building, especially because our company was used to a certain level of success and was still operating as if money were no object, wasting funds on power dinners and flights for meetings that could have easily happened over the phone.

Working from home, I managed twenty-three "distressed" malls in economically troubled markets. The stress was incredible. Part of my ambition and what drove me to do a good job was my love for people and my desire to bring comfort while still being smart and hitting the issues head on, but this issue really put me to the test. Every day, people asked me: Are we going to lose our jobs? Nobody knew the answer—not me, my boss, or my boss's boss. All I was supposed to do was manage the status quo, which was difficult for me because I'm not a status quo person. I'm motivated to achieve and maximize the potential of every situation. But it was hard enough just to keep people showing up to work every morning.

I participated in countless conference calls with my headset on. The only thing I could promise people who were barely hanging on to hope was that I would share with them all the information that I could share. I wouldn't keep any secrets, I told them, but if I were obligated to my boss not to divulge certain details, then I would have to keep my word. My people knew I was honorable and that I really did try to lead by example. I tried to walk the walk. But even as I attempted to be optimistic, my intuition told me that I should pre-pare them for the worst-case scenario. I walked them through the steps it would take to move on if they were let go, making sure they had backup plans. Instead of just spewing numbers and going on about budget cuts, I spent time on each person's individual needs. And while I did feel like this level of attention was part of my job, that's not why I did it. I did it because I genuinely cared about everyone on my team. I simply don't know how to deal with anyone in an impersonal manner.

When I got the call letting me know that I would

have to let go of twenty-three marketing directors across the country (out of 260 directors being fired companywide), I was sad but not surprised. What bothered me most was the way everyone was going to hear the news—via conference calls with their general managers. Severance packages aside, that seemed like a brutal way to say good-bye to valuable employees. I was very glad that I'd given my people that individual attention, and I knew they were prepared.

With my work life in such a state of chaos, I barely had any time or energy to think about men. But as far as my mother was concerned, the clock was still ticking. By the time I was forty-two, she and I had developed a very sincere and close relationship. She never said, "When are you getting married?" or "Maybe it's time to settle down." She would tell me that when I felt good about myself, it would happen. She was respectful of my choices and proud of my career. She was seeing me as an adult, not just as a daughter, and she always asked if it was okay for her to tell friends that I was single. I confided in her about everything—except for my shameful secret.

One day amid the upheaval at General Growth Properties, she excitedly called me to let me know that her friend at kickboxing class knew someone who'd be perfect for me. His name was John McNicholas, and he was a bankruptcy lawyer, my mother said, which piqued my interest—probably because there was so much talk of bankruptcy in the air. I agreed to meet him, but I tried not to get my hopes up too high. Blind dates, I'd learned, could be disastrous.

John, however, wasn't a disaster. We had so much in common that an online dating service probably would've matched us up right away. In addition to being a lawyer, John was an adjunct professor at Saint John's University. He lived in a beautiful apartment on Seventy-Eighth Street and Broadway in Manhattan. He was half Italian, half Irish, and grew up Catholic, like me. Neither one of us had ever been married, and we both were highly ambitious. In fact, we were so busy with work that it took us weeks to find time to get together. Finally, after several pleasant phone conversations and some schedule juggling, we made plans for dinner. I still remember exactly what I wore: a chocolate-brown wrap dress and tall, suede, high-heeled boots from Via Spiga. I'd just gotten my hair cut and colored. I was in good shape, and I was showing just a little bit of knee.

When John opened the door, he made me laugh right away. "I thought you were a blonde!" he said. We had never even seen pictures of each other.

"Why would you think that?" I asked him.

"I have no idea!" John was laughing at himself, too.

"Well, I hope you like brunettes!" I said, but I could tell from the look on his face that he did.

The rest of the night was just as easy and funny as those first moments were. We went around the corner from his place to a sushi restaurant, and I felt so comfortable around him that before long, one of my legs was draped over his. John wasn't phony or pretentious, which was refreshing in a man of his status. He loved to kid around, but he could be serious, too, and he wasn't afraid to be vulnerable. At one point, John set down his chopsticks and looked at me. He really is handsome, I thought.

"You know, Geri, I have to tell you something," he said.

Oh great, I thought. Here it comes. What's wrong with this one?

"A year ago, I would have never gone out with a girl like you," he said. "You're smart, and you're real. I didn't know a girl like you existed." John shook his head. "I was the stereotypical arrogant lawyer. I had no time for anybody but myself. Women came and went. They were nothing more than distractions. But then, my whole life changed."

I could tell from the look on his face that this wasn't going to be some off-the-wall story.

John said he was supposed to be going out on a date one night, when he started feeling sick. His date walked in the door, and he immediately had to go and lie down. Suddenly he couldn't feel his feet or legs, and the paralysis spread up his body, all the way up through his neck. He was unable to talk or breathe, and he was in a complete panic. His date called 911, and John was rushed to the hospital, where the news wasn't good. John was diagnosed with Guillain-Barré Syndrome, a rare disorder in which the body's immune system attacks the nerves. No one knows exactly what causes it or how to treat it. Though the severity of Guillain-Barré varies from patient to patient, John's case was particularly intense. He was hospitalized for months, and he actually died three times. Perhaps unsurprisingly, given the life-or-death nature of his experiences and the miracle of his recovery, John (like me) believed in angels and the divine. His favorite saint was John the Baptist. And he knew the real meaning of gratitude. He was thankful simply to be alive. Still, he managed to have a sense of humor about the whole thing.

"You wouldn't believe how many guys from work came and cried over me when I was in a coma, thinking I couldn't hear them," he said, laughing. "I wanted to say, 'You never cared about me before, asshole!'"

John was like me: we were both professionals who liked to work hard. We did not work extra hours for brownie points. His bosses appreciated him so much that they gave him a year off with pay. Not that it was a vacation—John still had serious work ahead, such as relearning how to walk.

By the time I met him, he was doing much better physically, though he may have been suffering post-traumatic shock from having a serious illness that had brought him to death's door. We were both in our forties, and it went unspoken that we were both ready for a serious relationship. I could tell that he felt safe with me from little things—like the way he asked me, midway through dinner, not to let him forget his black cashmere scarf. We had that kind of familiarity right away.

Unfortunately, I completely forgot to make sure John didn't forget his scarf that night. Neither one of us realized it until a few weeks later. We were seeing each other on a regular basis by then, and I was having so much fun. John still had enough of his old "arrogant lawyer" characteristics to be dynamic, but he was humble and kind, too.

One night when we were on the phone, John brought up the scarf. "Hey, did you happen to grab my black cashmere scarf for me that first night we went out?"

I'd completely forgotten about it, I told him.

"You were supposed to keep an eye on it for me," he said, teasing.

"I know, I'm so sorry," I said. "I guess I was distracted by a handsome man."

It was getting close to Christmastime, so I decided that a black cashmere scarf would make the perfect gift. Even though things were going really well with us, John and I wouldn't be spending Christmas together. We hadn't really been dating long enough to meet each other's families, particularly for a major holiday. But we still planned to exchange gifts. So, one night after work, I drove to Lord & Taylor to hunt for a black cashmere scarf. A nor'easter was in the forecast, but I figured it wouldn't take too long to find something as basic as a black cashmere scarf.

Lord & Taylor was deserted, so clearly everyone else in the area was taking the forecast seriously—and with good reason: within minutes, it was an absolute white-out outside. The snow was coming down fast and furiously. I got nervous and left after about twenty minutes without buying anything; oddly enough, I couldn't find a black cashmere scarf anywhere. My car was the only one in the parking lot, and the ground was completely covered in white—not a single footstep to be seen. As I walked to my car, a silver 1997 Mercedes, I saw something dark tied to the side mirror. When I got closer, I reached out to touch it—and stopped in my tracks.

It was a black cashmere scarf. I looked all around. My first thought was that John was hiding somewhere, playing a prank. But that didn't make sense because he had no idea that I was going to Lord & Taylor that evening to buy him a scarf, and he was nowhere to be seen. There was no trace of anyone anywhere. It simply didn't make sense.

I felt the fabric between my fingers and held the scarf to my nose. It smelled like a man, with just a hint of cologne clinging to it. Snow was falling heavily, so I got in my car and drove home carefully, completely baffled. I called John the minute I walked through the doorway.

"Where are you?" I asked.

"Home," he said. "It's looking bad out there."

"So, you're nowhere near my house? Or at Lord & Taylor?"

"What are you talking about?"

I told John what happened, even though it was going to ruin the surprise of my Christmas gift. He thought I was pulling his leg, and I didn't blame him. I wouldn't have believed it myself if it hadn't happened to me. Eventually, we laughed it off as a bizarre coincidence, even though I never stopped feeling that the scarf meant something.

I had other problems to deal with. One of the properties General Growth had acquired was New York City's South Street Seaport, which was undergoing a huge overhaul to include more retail stores and cater more to the tourist crowd. This historic spot came with a history of issues involving dissatisfied merchants, and General Growth Properties inherited a class-action lawsuit from the earlier owners stemming from these conflicts. John's law firm, DLA Piper, was handling the South Street Seaport lawsuit, which made things complicated for John and me.

He wasn't directly involved with the case, and I wasn't directly involved with the South Street Seaport property, but it still would have been unethical for us to talk about what the suit meant for my company. There were rumors flying that we were going to file for bankruptcy, and even though I wanted to know what John thought, I would never dream of asking. Thankfully, he found a way to warn me anyway.

"The market is a mess, Geri," he said. "That much I can tell you."

Just like I'd coached the members of my team in the weeks leading up to the layoffs, John helped me map out the possibilities and make a "just in case" plan. The first piece of advice he gave me was the most important: "if they offer you a field position, take it," he said.

"But that would be a demotion," I said. A field position meant moving to a mall location and managing it, instead of supervising a number of properties remotely as I was doing at the time.

"Believe me, it's your safest bet," said John.

Of course, that was the exact offer I got—or one of the offers. I was given two options. The first was to manage a nationwide program that had been around forever and, truth be told, really didn't need any managing. This would have allowed me to continue working from home, but it was also a "sitting duck" option. Since the position was practically unnecessary, it meant that I would be disposable. The second option was to manage the troubled Faneuil Hall Marketplace in Boston, another historic and beautiful property that was already struggling when we acquired it.

Boston? My heart sank. Not only would the new job be incredibly demanding and stressful because I'd have to operate as though GGP was on solid ground, it would also mean leaving John. I'd finally met a man who really meant something to me, a man who was open and funny and warm and believed in everything I believed in. How could I leave him behind? My first thought was that I would turn both offers down, start my consulting business—Geri Brown & Company, LLC—and (hopefully) marry John. But another part of me knew that our relationship was too new for that kind of pressure. After I got the call, I sat thinking in my apartment. I'd just finished renovating, putting in new crown molding and a wood floor that positively glowed. Everyone who came over to visit didn't want to leave. It wasn't a huge apartment, just 750 square feet, but I loved it. And it was finally exactly the way I wanted it. I had the home I wanted and the guy I wanted . . . but I knew I was going to leave.

John knew it, too. He knew I had no choice. He tried to make me feel better about it, even though I could tell he was hurting. John said he had an associate in Boston, and they'd been thinking about opening a practice in that city at some point.

"Who knows?" he said. "Maybe we'll have two offices, one in New York and one in Boston. We'll figure it out. You've got to take that job."

John gave me hope that we might actually have a future together, somehow, after our crazy lives got settled. He really was committed to my well-being, but it was too soon to commit beyond that.

Early in January, I got a call from GGP's corporate headquarters. All the vice presidents from around the country, including me, were going to be flown to Chicago for a meeting. I hung up the phone and stood there in silence. It was as if God spoke to me then, loud and clearly. I knew I had to move to Boston. My intuition was getting sharper as I got older. I was hearing things more clearly and listening to them.

At the meeting, all the vice presidents except me were let go. Not a single one was given the kind of offer I got, though some were given the opportunity to interview for field positions like mine. Some of the VPs broke down crying, though I'm pretty sure most of them didn't want to go to Faneuil Hall in Boston, either. But I had the qualifications and the right personality and energy for the job. Plus, unlike many of the other VPs, I was single and free to travel. I was not bound by the responsibilities of a family.

Which is not to say that my parents were happy about me going to Boston, of course. My mother was dumbfounded. Here she was thinking I'd met the love of my life, and now I was leaving him behind for my career. And she hated that I was moving away again, even though it was only a couple of hours away by car. Interestingly enough, I'd just taken my parents on a road trip to Boston when I went to help a former intern who'd been promoted to work on the Faneuil Hall property and was feeling in over her head. My mother had taken magnificent pictures there, and my parents enjoyed the city. I knew they would miss me, but they'd also be happy to visit.

* * *

I arrived in Boston on the day the New England Patriots lost the Super Bowl to the New York Giants—in other words, the last day anybody in Boston wanted to see a New Yorker. As the first female general manager of Faneuil Hall Marketplace, I'd oversee a team that included a sixty-four-year-old operations director and a bunch of burly Irish guys who didn't seem too enthusiastic about being bossed around by a little girl from New York. I knew I had to do something to get those people on my side.

The problem was, they were already suspicious of me. When our company took over Faneuil Hall, it hadn't done a proper job of introducing the CEO to the mayor of Boston, Thomas Menino. This caused a long-standing rift. Then there were the merchants, who hoped that General Growth Properties would save them from the fallout of the previous owner's attempts to incorporate more local artisans into the marketplace. Many locals had praised this shift in direction for its "charm," but ultimately, it didn't generate enough income to cover the accompanying improvements in the structure and other updates. Those same locals were still up in arms over the subsequent addition of more national chains like Gap and Victoria's Secret. So, there was no way of making everyone happy.

Faneuil Hall and the Merchant's Association were very tight, and there was very little turnover, so these people had been working together for a long time. They were already frustrated by false promises when General Growth Properties came along. And unfortunately, since then, things had only gotten worse, not better. This was due in part to the fact that we were also building a big, beautiful new shopping center with condos in Natick, a suburb of Boston. The mayor of Boston was upset that all General Growth Properties' energy seemed to be focused on this new development, and understandably so.

I arrived in Boston knowing some of this; still, the depth of bad feelings came as quite a shock. Things got even worse a year later when I got a phone call from corporate saying they weren't sure if they would be able to pay back the loans they'd gotten to purchase the property. They were filing for bankruptcy protection, and they'd put Faneuil Hall up for sale. On and on it went. Over the course of the next year, I tried everything I could to put things right.

To get calm, I'd go to mass, sometimes running to Saint Anthony's Shrine on Arch Street, less than a mile away, while my secretary covered for me. Other times, I went to Saint Stephen's Church on Hanover Street. One day, I spoke to an old Irish priest there. I confided in him about the corruption at Faneuil Hall and told him that I didn't know what to do. He gave me a book on meditation. It is in that state, he said, when you are calm and clear, that you can hear God.

One event that did pull everyone together at Faneuil Hall was the opening of the Rose Kennedy Greenway, a series of linear gardens and parks connecting some of Boston's oldest neighborhoods. The parks are on land that Boston "reclaimed" during the Big Dig, in which the city's elevated highways were replaced by a system of tunnels. I convinced the Faneuil Hall merchants that we should support events like that one and the Italian Festival in the North End because by giving, we would receive. The greenway opening was wildly successful for us because we all worked together. We put interns in T-shirts commemorating Rose Kennedy, the mother of President John F. Kennedy, and they handed out pink roses donated by our merchants.

At the black-tie dinner for the greenway opening, I sat next to children's author-illustrator Peter H. Reynolds, whose book *Rose's Garden* was animated and played at the event on a giant video screen. I knew Peter as the author of *The Dot*, a children's book about encouraging creativity. As we talked at dinner, he drew a sketch of me on the back of his program. I was watering a plant. *Keep on connecting the dots!* he wrote underneath it. He was a delightful dinner companion, and his note gave me a real lift.

Still, at Faneuil Hall, I met obstacles at almost every turn. It was crucial to repair GGP's image in Boston, but most of the time it felt like the public-relations people were working against us, not for us. I saw backstabbing tactics I never even dreamed possible. To my face, it was always, "Geri, these are great ideas!" Then they'd go to the press and slam General Growth Properties.

To be fair, GGP wasn't handling any of it well, and I was constantly being put in positions that made me uncomfortable. One such incident was a meeting at Mayor Menino's office on Ash Wednesday. Faneuil Hall merchants were ganging up on GGP, saying that the company wasn't managing the mall properly, and complaining to the mayor that we were turning it into a "regular" mall by leasing space to national chains who can afford the higher rent. Even though some of the unique artisans who also had space there could no longer afford the rent and had stopped paying.

I knew I was in for yet another battle that day, and my boss would have his tail between his legs. So, I went to church before the meeting and walked into the mayor's office with ashes on my forehead. I could sense that people around the meeting table were surprised. But that was a Joan of Arc moment for me. I needed protection, and I wore it right on my face.

I was so disgusted with how two-faced and dishonest people could be that I was on the verge of a nervous breakdown. Since I'd been in Boston, it was like a dark shadow had been cast over my life. I was so wrapped up in the drama that I was losing touch with myself. The indicator was that my back started to act up again.

That's when I got the call at work.

"Geraldine?" It was my mother. I could tell right away from her voice that something was wrong.

"Mom, what's the matter?"

"I don't know how to tell you this," my mother said. "I'm so sorry, Geraldine, but John died."

A wave of shock and grief hit me full force. John was

163

dead? How was that possible? I frantically searched my memory, trying to recall the last time we spoke and what he had said. We hadn't talked for a while, not because of any kind of falling out or lack of desire but because we'd both been so extremely busy. John's mother had been ill, and he was back at work full-time, so his year had been physically and emotionally draining, too. But I never thought I wouldn't see or talk to him again. There would always be time, we thought. Apparently, we were wrong.

"I'm so sorry, Geraldine," my mother said again.

I went home that night feeling completely defeated, as low as I'd ever felt. I would never really hurt myself, but I'd be lying if I said it didn't cross my mind to jump out the window or step in front of a moving truck on my way home to the North End. If ever there were a time for me to give up, this would have been it.

Out of the blue, a few days later, I got a call from Robin Miller, an outside consultant we'd used for holiday decor. We'd hit it off years before, and we'd had many conversations about faith. As I told Robin about everything that was going on, all the hostility and failures, I broke down crying. The weight of it all, especially John's loss, just felt so heavy.

"Geri," Robin said to me, her voice soft. "You're swimming in toxic waters. You need to get out."

It was like my guardian angel speaking to me through this woman. Her voice on the phone gave me the first small measure of comfort I'd felt in a long time, and I knew she was right.

Strangely enough, former President Richard Nixon

had given me similar advice when I'd met him by chance more than two decades earlier. I'd accompanied Stan, Paige, and Rebecca to Key Biscayne, Florida, where Nixon lived in retirement. Rebecca and I were making jewelry at our resort's kids' camp when a little boy came over to us and said, "Hey, do you want to meet the president of the United States?"

"President Reagan?" I asked, naming the current occupant of the Oval Office.

"No," he said, "President Nixon."

Intrigued, we followed him into another room at the resort, where Nixon was sitting, surrounded by his Secret Service detail. We walked right up to him, and I said, "Hello, Mr. President."

He and I chatted easily for a few minutes, and then he said, "Young lady, do me a favor. Stay out of the sun. Otherwise, you'll get burned and end up like me." At the time, I thought he was referring to his suntanned and wrinkled face. Now, however, I thought about the political implications of *getting burned*, which was exactly what I was enduring at Faneuil Hall.

Even though it was cold outside, I went for a walk along Boston Harbor on my way to work the next morning. I needed to collect my thoughts. I couldn't bring myself to go into my office. I couldn't think of anywhere I really wanted to go. Did I even want to be in Boston at all?

It's not that living in Boston was all bad. My apartment was gorgeous and right on the water. It was my oasis of peace and comfort. There was a private pool just across the street. I used to swing on the swing set there in the moonlight. On weekends, I'd ride my bike along the Charles River. I had happy memories of my place, which I'd tried to make into a home. I always had fresh cut flowers in vases and spent far too much money hosting dinners for my friends. There was a beautiful rooftop deck with a view of the harbor. But why was I experiencing all this all alone?

My internal crisis coincided with a looming choice. My landlord had put my apartment on the market after he found out General Growth Properties was going bankrupt, so if I wanted to stay, I'd have to buy it. I had the means, but for some reason, I was still terrified of making such a huge investment on my own. I'd put off the decision for a while because, in the back of my head, I was thinking that maybe John and I would get married. But now I had to face the fact that I was truly on my own, and this choice was no one else's to make.

Sitting on the bench at the harbor that morning, I needed advice. I couldn't talk to Mom about it; she'd sympathize, but she'd never experienced a workplace like mine. I couldn't talk to my boss; I doubted he'd understand how I felt. So, I called Arianna Fuccini, my life coach in Boston.

She was the second life coach I'd consulted. The first, a woman named Claire of Claire Light Coaching, had helped me get straightened out financially by saving and investing in a home before I'd moved to Boston. Now, I confided to Arianna that I didn't know whether to stay with GGP.

"I don't know where to go. I don't know what to do," I said, watching the waves roll out to sea.

Arianna had been rooting for me to fix the mess at Faneuil Hall, but now it was evident that the stress was taking a big toll on my mind, body, and soul. "I think you need to go home," she said.

It was a humble moment, realizing that I could not conquer the problems at Faneuil Hall. But my intuition told me she was right, and the way the universe cooperated with this choice only confirmed it. Serendipitously, the tenant who'd been leasing my apartment in Scarsdale was leaving at the same time I needed to get back in. With housing taken care of, I needed to figure out how to handle my departure from General Growth Properties. With the help of a lawyer, I sent a letter detailing my reasons for leaving and what I deserved as compensation. I ended up getting what I thought was a fair severance package.

Back in Westchester, I was relieved to be away from the stress of my previous job, but I was heartbroken. I had believed in GGP's commitment to its employees, and leaving the company felt like a divorce. I felt so lost, so out of touch with the person I'd been and the person I was meant to be. I started taking long bike rides down the Bronx River Parkway to clear my mind.

One day, as I circled my favorite duck pond on my bike, I was frustrated and sad and at a loss. I needed help. I needed something to keep me going, and I found myself praying to John.

"John, you know me," I prayed. "You know my heart. Please, can you help me out and send me someone? The right someone?"

Just then, I noticed that something was wrong with

one of my tires—the brake seemed to be sticking—so I pulled over and sat down on a bench to check it out. That's when I saw them: tied to the bench was a black cashmere scarf, just like John's black cashmere scarf. And sitting right next to it was a toy frog.

Fully rely on God, I thought. If I'd been sitting on my bike, I would've fallen over. I was in shock. Something told me to pick up the frog and flip it over. On the bottom of the frog were the letters MCNC, with a cross and the number 43. John McNicholas died on April 2, but I'd always imagined him rising to Heaven on April 3—4/3.

As I sat there holding the frog, Aretha Franklin came through my earbuds singing the classic Burt Bacharach/Hal David tune "I Say a Little Prayer."

I looked up at the sky with tears in my eyes, knowing that John was with me.

Chapter Fourteen

Freewheeling

I always said the toughest part of working out is lacing up your sneakers. At forty-nine years old, I was lucky. Other women my age looked at exercise as some form of punishment, but for me, every moment I spent on my bike was as exhilarating and joyful as it was when I was a little girl. When I was pushing myself really hard, my muscles burning and my forehead shining with sweat, I didn't care what I looked like. I'd crank up my special bike-ride playlist on my iPod and coast along with both hands in the air, dancing like I was at a club on a Saturday night. People would stop and stare at me like I was a trick rider in a rodeo, but it didn't bother me one bit if strangers thought I was wild. With Fergie from the Black-Eyed Peas singing "Boom, boom, boom" in my ears, endorphins coursing through my blood, and the wind in my face, I was free. I wasn't forty-nine; I was nine years old—and loving every minute of it.

My girlfriend Gerri had convinced me to try online dating when I moved back to Westchester County from Boston, and I worked out my online profile as I sped along the Hudson River on those bike rides. "Never having been married doesn't bother me because I believe that my soul will connect with the right person at the right time of my life," I wrote in that profile. "In the meantime, I have a ball, loving life, my family, friends, and work, and helping others as much as I possibly can. My time is spent traveling, running and exercising, being near water, eating well, living honestly, working hard, and seeing the beauty in everything." I was totally honest.

But the men I met online were disappointing. I wanted a man who was comfortable in his own skin, but what I met were guys who hid their baldness with toupées and used decade-old photos online to suggest that they were younger than their actual years.

One guy I dated thought I was a fashion diva. He loved the way I dressed. "I saw an outfit in Manhattan that's perfect for you," he'd say. Then, one day, he took me out on his boat. I fell asleep in the sun, and when I woke up, he was wearing my makeup.

Yikes!

After the miraculous scarf and frog sighting at the duck pond, I'd not only started to look for signs that a man was right for me, but I'd also started taking a serious look at the things I didn't like about myself. I spent a lot of time in contemplation, trying to figure out what I needed to do differently to make room for love in my life. I believed that it was on its way. I just didn't know the details.

* * *

Philip wasn't the kind of guy anyone expected me to date. He was sweet and adorable and kind, but he was also short and round and fifty-eight years old.

I met him through work. When I'd moved back to Scarsdale, I'd discovered that an outdoor shopping center was being developed about four and a half miles from my home. Bruce Ratner, of Forest City Ratner, who had built the Barclays Center in Brooklyn, was the principal. I called and met with his marketing executive and asset-management team. A week after that two-hour interview, I was on the payroll as a marketing consultant. My job included setting up concerts in the parking lot.

Philip was the sound engineer for those events, and we always had a good time working together, but I never thought about him romantically. He thought about me, though.

"Hey, Geri," he finally said one day. "Would you ever let me take you out for a ride on my motorcycle?" There was something almost shy about the way he asked. It touched me.

"Anytime, Philip," I said. "All you have to do is ask."

Sitting behind Philip on his bike, the wind blowing through my hair, I started to enjoy myself. Every now and then, he would turn around and crack a joke or give my arm a squeeze. Maybe I should give this guy a chance, I thought.

Philip turned out to be the kind of man who would do anything for anyone, especially me. I was having a lot of anxiety about my job, starting to spread myself a little too thin again. Having someone to take care of me, for once, was exactly what I needed at the time. And the benefits of our relationship went both ways: while we were dating, Philip lost sixty pounds—not by exercising or dieting or doing anything on purpose, but just because he was happy. And, I suppose, my healthy habits were rubbing off on him. Exercise was more important to me than ever and eating right had always been part of my lifestyle.

There was one very unhealthy habit that was hanging over my head, though, and that was smoking. I'd been a smoker on and off for years, and I was incredibly annoyed with myself because I'd quit before, but I started up again when I got back from Boston. My father (a lifelong smoker) had already been through skin and kidney and throat cancer. I called him "the warrior" because he taught me what resilience really means. I'd even had my own cancer scare in 2013, having a partial hysterectomy for a grapefruit-sized mass in one ovary. These things should have been enough to make me stay away from cigarettes. But, like so many others, I went back.

What was wrong with me? I hated the way my mouth tasted like cigarettes every time I had a smoke; I hated the antsy feeling I would get when it had been too long since my last one. I hated being dependent on anything, especially something that was bad for me. But I couldn't seem to bring myself to stop. I knew that it wasn't a habit, it was an addiction.

One night, Philip and I went to the movies to see

Whiplash, the award-winning film about a gifted music student and his demanding professor. The main character was a drummer who threw himself so passionately into his art that he would practice until his hands bled. I was incredibly moved by the film and the fiery commitment of the main character.

"Philip, when was the last time you really gave something your all?" I asked as we walked out of the theater.

"What do you mean?" Philip smiled, sensing that I had something big on my mind.

"You know, when was the last time you really threw yourself into something like that kid in the movie did?" I asked. "Like all of you, every inch. Gave your ultimate all."

Philip thought for a moment. "Well, I don't know," he said finally. "But I bet you do."

Philip was right. I did know. I remembered perfectly the last time I attacked something with that level of gusto, and it was in fourth grade. I told Philip about how my mom and dad used to take us to a winter carnival out on Lake Lincolndale where there were activities like ice skating and ice softball games. The year I was nine, I decided to compete in an ice-skating tournament. We were put into co-ed groups, divided by age, and then each group circled the pond a few times before a round of kids was eliminated. I remember hearing the blades of my skates scraping against the ice on the final, suspenseful turn. I was thrilled when I made it to the semifinals—until I came down with a classic case of nerves. Drinking a paper cup of hot chocolate and waiting for the next round to begin, I told my mother I had an earache and wanted to go home.

My mother was no fool. This wasn't the first time I'd given her the earache excuse. It had been an ongoing joke since I suddenly came down with an imaginary one before it was my turn to go onstage during a Christmas pageant. I was dressed like a tree in green tights and my cousin's green dress, and I was nervous. My mother came backstage, put her mouth to my ear, and whispered, "Just pray the rosary; you'll be fine." That distraction had worked, so this time, my mother put her hands on the shoulders of my puffy brown jacket and looked me in the eyes.

"Geraldine, you know you don't have an earache. You're just going to put your head down and skate and do your very best. That's all you can do."

The next thing I remember is the starting pistol firing and the smell of the gunpowder in the crisp winter air. I did what my mother said and kept my head down. I skated and skated and never looked up . . . and before I knew what had happened, I had won the race! I was stunned. But I never forgot that feeling of triumph and how it meant even more to me because I'd worked so hard for it. That was the moment I learned I could do anything if I gave it my all.

I decided to put my mind to quitting smoking the same way I'd put my mind to winning that race. Every time I felt like giving in, I remembered that moment on the frozen lake and the smell of gunpowder in the air. I threw out my last pack of cigarettes and instead of lighting up, I thought about why I smoked in the first place. A cigarette was my escape whenever I was in a stressful situation, a way to avoid the anger or sadness I was feeling. It was an excuse to stop and think, a reward for cleaning the house or doing the laundry. But most of all, smoking was a way to hide, especially from myself. The time for that was gone, I knew. I had to learn to accept myself and truly love myself if I was ever going to find love.

I did quit smoking, but I also realized that Philip was not the great love I was looking for. He was a lovely, compassionate person, and he was good to me. He was with me when I underwent the partial hysterectomy. It had never occurred to me before that I wouldn't have children, but now, I had to face that fact. The realization was devastating. It compounded the sorrow I carried deep inside. Philip held me and cried with me. He knew the bonds I had with my nieces and nephews, and he knew how much I loved children.

Still, he and I weren't cut from the same cloth. There was someone out there, I knew, who was meant for me and someone else who was perfect for Philip. To me, this was clear. Philip, on the other hand, was happier than he'd ever been in his life, and he associated that happiness with me. With his weight loss and his elevated mood, his self-esteem had improved, and he was more confident. He even started going to church again. I worried that I would burst his bubble or undo all the progress he'd made by breaking up with him.

My family had also gotten close to Philip, which only made my decision more difficult. He was an honorable man and had easily won them over with his warmth and good-natured spirit. Before too long he was calling my parents Mom and Dad. When he lost me, he'd be losing his new family, too.

Philip wanted to take me on vacation. I wanted to say no, but I was still holding on to the very slim hope that something might shift in my heart. So, we went to the Caribbean together. It should have been an amazing trip, but I couldn't have felt more uncomfortable. Everybody we hung out with was approaching sixty, and I had no one to join me in any fun physical activities. These people were talking about retirement and grandchildren, and I was still thinking about my next career moves and wondering if I would ever get married. These were not my people. Philip and I both knew it, but we didn't want to talk about it. We were supposed to be in paradise. I was temperamental, too, partly because I was still adjusting to not being a smoker. All my hidden emotions were out on the table, and I felt raw and vulnerable. I wanted to beg him not to get me a ring for my birthday, which was coming up.

Easter was coming up, too. Sitting in the confessional at church after we got back from our awkward vacation, I opened up to Father Farley about my dilemma.

"He's such a good person, Father," I said. "I just don't know what to do."

Father Farley told me to pray to Saint Joseph, the protector of the family. Saint Joseph was a kind, compassionate, and strong father figure. He would guide me to the right man, Father said.

As was my custom when I had something weighing on my mind, I went for a long bike ride one morning in

June. With the bright green trees and shimmering blue water whizzing past, I was feeling even more contemplative than usual. It was God's voice I was hoping to hear that day as I rode in the direction of Our Lady of Fatima Church. So, you can imagine my reaction when suddenly, in between The Black-Eyed Peas and the Red Hot Chili Peppers, a man's voice came booming through my headphones: "In the name of the Father, the Son, and the Holy Spirit."

I nearly fell off my bike. *Is that you, God?* It took me a minute to remember that I'd recently uploaded the audio guide on praying the rosary to my iPod. I'd completely forgotten it was on the playlist when I set it to "shuffle" at the beginning of my ride. The Our Father was quite a departure from "Boom, Boom, Pow." Once I calmed down, though, I got right into the groove of praying as I pumped my legs up and down: One Our Father, one Hail Mary, one Glory Be, then the Hail Mary three times (for faith, hope, and charity). Praying along with the recording was soothing and helped me to focus.

When I slowed my bike to a stop in front of the statue of the Blessed Virgin Mary, Our Lady of Fatima, I looked up and saw that someone had put a wreath of roses on her head. My heart fluttered in my chest. Roses always made me think of my grandma Rosaria.

I gazed at Mary's still, serene face and implored her directly from my heart.

"Blessed Mother," I prayed. "If I'm single, that's okay. If that's what you and God want for me, I can accept being alone as my calling. If I am single, I just want to be happy. But if I'm married, I have this list of things I want in a man . . ."

When I went home, I dug up my old list of the "Fifty Things I Want in a Man" and looked it over for the first time in a long time. All the things I'd listed—loving God, being youthful in spirit, being open-minded and patient—were still important to me, but for the first time, I considered what it might be like if I never found the theoretical man I described on the list. I was successful, I had friends, I had my faith. I had the ability to find joy in situations so many other people couldn't. And I knew that whether that man existed or not, I could still have a fulfilling and wonderful life. I already did.

I was a successful single, and I was not afraid of being alone. Philip was a lovely person, but he was not "the one" for me, and I realized that it wasn't fair of me to hold onto him.

When I broke up with him, he was absolutely devastated. It went horribly, but he didn't push things. He backed off right away. But when my father's birthday came along, Philip called me and asked if he could come to the family party. He'd gotten close to my parents, and I knew they missed him, too, so I said okay.

He met me at my parents' house, and things went as smoothly as they could. I spent most of my time indoors with my younger brother, Richie, and his three kids, while Philip and my father hung out outside. Then, suddenly, my mother's good friend Eunice came barreling through the house into the kitchen.

"Teresa, Teresa," she called out to my mother. "Have

I got a man for Geraldine!"

Eunice and my mother had been friends for twenty-four years. She was thoughtful and filled with spirit and always dropped by with a rich, decadent, beautifully decorated little cake on my parents' birthdays. She was also funny and brash, and her voice could carry for miles.

"Shhh, Eunice!" My mother looked out the window at Philip nervously. "Geraldine has her 'friend' here!"

My eleven-year-old niece Mia's ears perked up. I hadn't told anyone in my family besides my mother that I'd broken up with Philip.

"What's going on?" Mia asked.

"Nothing, nothing," my mother said, shooting Eunice a look.

Eunice dropped the subject, but later, the three of us had a moment alone together.

"So, tell me about this guy," said my mother. "Who is he? Where do you know him from?"

"His boat is docked next to mine—" Eunice said, but I interrupted her with one word.

"Boat?" It was like a little light switch flipped on in my heart. I wasn't sure why, but something about a boat sounded so right. I thought about all the times I'd invited younger coworkers over to take clothes when I cleaned out my closet. For years, I'd had a pair of boat shoes from Lord & Taylor that I didn't wear, but if someone expressed interest in them, I'd say, "No, those have to stay. Hands off!" *Hmm* . . .

I didn't say anything else as Eunice spoke. I just sat there with a big smile on my face and listened. His name was Mark, and he worked for IBM, Eunice said. He was about my age, in good shape, and handsome, too, she assured me.

"And he's such a doll," she said.

"Eunice, they're fifty years old," said my mother. "You stay out of it!"

"She can exchange numbers with him. What's the big deal?" Eunice wanted to know.

So, I put Mark's number into my phone. What could it hurt? Something sparked in me that I hadn't felt in a long time—that hope and excitement that comes when the potential for love shows up. Granted, I'd never even seen Mark. But that wasn't the point. The point was that I felt a door slowly start to open in the universe somewhere. I wasn't going to push it open, but I wasn't going to slam it closed, either. I was just going to walk through that doorway when the time was right.

Chapter Fifteen

Meeting with Destiny

In the past, the prospect of meeting a new man might have made me anxious. But as intrigued as I was by the idea of Mark, I didn't feel the need to rush into meeting him. I just tried to be present in every moment of my life and waited for the right moment, trusting I would know when it was time. He had told Eunice that he'd like to see a photo of me, so after she left my dad's birthday party, I sent one. But instead of choosing a picture of me all dressed up with my hair done, I sent him a shot of my nieces and me on the beach in Maine, all bundled up in towels. In the accompanying text message, I wrote:

> *With my nieces in Bar Harbor . . .*
> *Luv them they are the best!*
>
> *PS Auntie in the middle . . . Safe*
> *travels.*

Mark replied:

> *Nice pic! Sry I'm in a very bad cell*
> *area. Can't even make a call—I'll*

> *check with you when I get back to*
> *CT*

Then I didn't hear from him for several weeks. But that silence didn't bother me. I was busy. I had changed jobs again—I'd left my job at the outdoor mall to make room for something else, though I had no idea what that would be. It was a bold, life-altering decision, but I felt strongly that I needed a new direction and I needed to take some time to meditate and work on myself.

Meanwhile, I was on the board of directors for the YMCA in White Plains. When a marketing position opened at the Y, I took it despite the pay cut it represented.

Sitting in my new office, thinking about my new life, I looked at the photo I'd sent to Mark and noticed that the sunlight reflecting off my niece's towel looked like an angel. On an impulse, I texted him:

> *Hi there, how's boat life treating*
> *you?*

I wasn't obsessed with waiting for his reply. A few days later, I was getting into my car when my phone pinged with a text message. It was from Mark.

> *Hi Geri,*
>
> *Underway with the boat—Txt you*
> *later on or in the am, thx for con-*
> *tacting me.*
>
> *Have you heard from your aunt*
> *recently?*

I replied:

No haven't she has been ships ahoy

Mark replied that he knew my mom's friend Eunice and her husband were off boating, because they docked their boat next to his. Then, he added:

Was just thinking about you yester-day.

I wrote:

Our thoughts collided I guess.

Mark replied:

:)

I discovered that I enjoyed working in the nonprofit sector, and I was training for our annual fundraising campaign, which involved absorbing a large amount information in a very short span of time. That training took me to Syracuse, New York.

The morning after the training session ended, I decided to go to the church next door to my hotel. My flight home would not leave until afternoon, and I just had a feeling that something was happening. Something was shifting in my life. When I got there, I realized there was no morning mass, but the doors were open. So, I went inside and knelt in one of the many empty pews. In the quiet of the church, I went back to the place in my heart where I'd been the day I'd ridden my bike to the statue of Our Lady of Fatima.

"If I'm meant to be single, then help me to be okay," I prayed. "And if I'm not, please let the person I meet truly understand me and what I'm all about."

When I went back to my hotel room to pack, I noticed for the first time that every piece of art on the walls depicted roses. I even had one of the prints at home. I thought of the roses around my grandma Rosaria's statue of the Blessed Mother of God and her devotion to Saint Thérèse, the Little Flower. I could feel my grandmother's presence in the room, as if she was saying hello, and that made me calm. When I flew into JFK that afternoon, my car service was delayed, but I didn't mind because the sunset at that particular moment looked so glorious reflected in the airport windows. I even took a photo of it. I felt completely at peace. (Oddly enough, I would learn later that Mark had photographed the same sunset that day in Montauk.)

I was exhausted when I got home that evening, so I took the next day off. One of the best things about my job at the Y was the flexibility. I was only making half of what I'd made at the shopping center, but I'd negotiated five weeks of time off on top of holidays, and I was able to take my vacation days anytime I wanted.

The next day, Friday, was beautiful, with a perfect weekend in the forecast. I went for a twenty-mile bike ride, then I went to an energy yoga class. I had my nails done and got the car washed, and by midafternoon, I was browsing at Barnes & Noble. I've always loved the smell of books and the air of creativity that permeates book stores. That night, I decided, I'd have a date with myself at my favorite restaurant, Harvest on the Hudson, and on Saturday, I'd head to Robert Moses Beach to soak up some sun and ride some waves. I was in a fabulous mood.

Suddenly, my phone pinged. It was Mark resuming our conversation:

> *Hello—I'm in MTK Alone—*
>
> *If you can make it out here for the weekend you can stay with me. I have an extra bunk on the boat. There's tons of People around that Know me so your Safe—*
>
> *—Mark*
>
> *I'm a total gentleman so no worries there either. I have my car out here also—so it's sunrises, beaches, nice restaurants, sunsets and star filled nights*

I was intrigued—no, I was blown away! But I wanted to make sure he knew that I was not into playing games. I also wanted to hear his voice. So, I texted back:

> *What?? Can we talk on the phone?! I'm a true beach bum . . . And fish so don't put the bait out unless very serious (SMILEY FACE)*

Mark called a few minutes later, and a warm feeling

washed over me when I heard him. I liked his voice. By that point, my biggest reservation was the traffic. On summer Fridays, it seemed that all of New York City would head to the Hamptons on Long Island, and locals and tourists alike called Montauk "the End"—the last stop. Under perfect conditions, the two-hundred-mile trip would take three and a half hours, but in rush-hour traffic on a Friday, I knew it would take five or six hours. I'd be lucky if I made it out there by midnight.

"I completely understand if you don't want to make the drive tonight, and if you want to come out in the morning, that's fine with me," Mark said. "But I'm just going to say one thing: you can't beat waking up on the water."

That was enough for me. I packed a bag (after he assured me there were showers at the marina). I got dressed in an outfit I thought was the right mix of stylish and casual: white shorts with a little cuff, a burgundy silk tank top from Eileen Fisher, a pale beige cashmere cardigan, and cute neutral-colored shoes. My hair was in a high ponytail, and I was wearing just a little bit of makeup. My legs were toned and tan from my frequent bike rides, and I felt healthy and confident. For some reason, even though I was getting ready to spend the weekend with a man I was interested in, I wasn't worried about what I looked like. And when I hit the highway, I stopped worrying about traffic, too. It was as if the Long Island Expressway had simply opened up for me.

Most Friday nights, the roads out to Montauk from Westchester looked like a parking lot. But that night, it was smooth sailing.

I knew where I was going, so I allowed my thoughts to drift as I drove. I wasn't making any assumptions about what I was about to encounter—I wasn't even wondering about what Mark would look like in person. I was more interested in who he was as a spiritual being. As I got closer, I stopped to text and let him know where I was. He was shocked.

"Wow. I better shower," he texted back.

Then, when I got to the marina, I called him. "I'm here," I said.

With a smile in his voice, he said, "I hope you don't mind gray hair!"

"That's just fine with me," I said.

The sun was almost down. I'd left home at 5:10 p.m. and it was not yet 8:30. The Long Island Expressway had simply parted like the Red Sea. I opened the door of my white Kia Sportage and slipped my leg out first to give Mark a little preview of what he was getting from wherever he was watching.

He came up from behind and took my hand. I stood up and looked at him, and we just smiled at each other. I loved his face from the first moment I saw it. He had beautiful white teeth and a cleft in his chin—one of my top-fifty things! At around five-foot nine, he was just shy of the height requirement on my list. (I mentally shifted that trait from the "must have" to the "would like" category in my mind.) The most important thing was that when I looked into his eyes, it was like I was looking into the eyes of someone I'd known my whole life. Except, it was better, because there was all the hope and promise that comes with a new relationship, too.

We were right at the water's edge, and the lights from the marina glittered on the surface of the ocean. Mark helped me get the bags out of the back of my car and led me down the gravel driveway past a park with a gazebo to the wooden dock where all the boats were lined up. Sportsman's Dock Marina was intimate, only about fifty or so boats total. Most of them were perpendicular to the dock in their individual slips, but not Mark's. His forty-five-foot Viking was parallel to the dock at the very end, all by itself, so there was no obstruction to the spectacular ocean view. I would find out later that Marie and Bob, the marina owners, adored Mark, and when they saw how determined he was to pull out the stops for my visit, they offered him that prime spot with the priceless view.

Mark took my hand again as we stepped down on to the boat, which was even better than I expected. I had my own little guest stateroom right next to the bathroom, with a cute blanket that read "Montauk" on it. There was a little kitchen and a comfortable couch. I noticed right away that everything was immaculate, and it didn't have that stuffy sort of smell some boats get. I felt comfortable right away, and it dawned on me that the inside of Mark's boat reminded me of my own apartment, with the coconut-cream-colored upholstery and glowing, golden woodwork. I put my things away in my room, and Mark and I sank down next to each other on the couch.

"I want you to know something," Mark said. "I had the whole interior of this boat redone after my divorce."

I knew that Mark was divorced and had no children, but I didn't know much about his marriage or why it ended. That didn't bother me, though. With another man, a looming question mark like that might have nagged at me, but I didn't pick up on any kind of lingering vibe. I didn't sense another woman's presence in any way.

"I wanted to clear out the old to make way for the new," he said and smiled.

Looks like it worked, I thought.

Since I'd managed to arrive so early, we still had time to go out for dinner. The restaurant was across the harbor, so we took Mark's car. This time, we walked down the dock arm in arm, and we fit together perfectly. We drove to a beautiful restaurant a few miles past the downtown area called Inlet Seafood. It was known for having the best seafood in Montauk, Mark told me.

"You've never had sushi like this, believe me," he said.

Even though it was one of the busiest spots in town on a Friday night, we managed to get a table outside on the patio. The word *romantic* doesn't even begin to do justice to the setting. As we sat down, the last of the blue sky was melding into the pink horizon. The soft sea breeze, the starlight . . . the scene was straight out of a movie. And yet, I didn't feel any pressure. I felt completely at ease.

We ordered drinks and started talking, the way you do on a first date, about our backgrounds and interests and jobs. But none of it felt like small talk, and nothing felt forced. I was asking Mark questions I really wanted to know the answers to, not just spinning my conversational wheels while I secretly wondered what kind of a guy he was. The gleam Mark got in his eye when he spoke—especially about one of his passions, like boating—completely captivated me. I wasn't surprised to hear that he grew up in Connecticut, spending most of his summers on the water; he seemed so knowledgeable about everything nautical. He had the kind of self-assurance that came with being smart and accomplished, but he was humble, too. He didn't brag about the things he'd done or what he had; he shared his stories with me out of genuine excitement. It was infectious and mesmerizing.

As we spoke, our heads tipped toward each other's, I had my hand on the table with my palm open. Mark started making a circle in the palm of my hand with his finger, very gently. It was more affectionate than sexual, a gesture that seemed to connect us on a deeper level. Suddenly I had a flashback to Joe George, making the circle with his finger on the airport table.

For a moment, I lost track of what Mark was saying as I tried to recall exactly what Joe George had told me. His three key points had been that I would receive a gift, that I should never lose the little girl inside of me, and that my grandmother had something to tell me and I should trust myself to know when I heard it. Was this the message my grandmother had promised to send? All those feelings and the years of questioning came rushing back, stirring up something buried way down inside me. I felt a burning heat all over. I started sweating profusely. Even my ankles were sweating, and I had no idea that ankles could sweat!

Then I realized that I was, in fact, having a hot flash. I grabbed a menu and started fanning myself with it. "Look," I told Mark. "Don't think you're so hot. This is what they call a hot flash."

Mark roared with laughter. Never in my life did I ever imagine that a moment like this one could be so funny. I wasn't the least bit embarrassed.

"Geraldine," Mark said, "there are three things you need to know about me."

"Okay, shoot," I said.

"First, if you tell me something, sometimes it goes in one ear and out the other." He made a funny motion with his hand to demonstrate. "So, you'll have to be patient with me."

"Okay, I can handle that," I said. "What else?"

"Second, I'm all heart," he said.

"I can definitely handle that," I said.

"Good," he said. "The other thing is, I'm a guy, so you're going to have to give me a few mulligans here and there."

The funny thing was, I only knew what mulligans were because I'd been doing fundraising for the Y and Doris, the secretary, had explained to me recently that in golf terms, a mulligan was a do-over.

When we got into the car to leave, Mark turned to me.

"There's something very special about you," he said. "So, I want to take you to a really special place."

I was ready for anything. Mark said he was going

to take me to see Camp Hero, a beautiful state park on Montauk Point, about five miles from the center of town. It's a famous landmark that was commissioned by the U.S. Army in 1942 and later used as an air force station, but I didn't know about it—I kept thinking that Mark was saying *Campiro*. Whatever it was called, it was breathtaking, he said, and he wanted to take me out to the bluffs. When we pulled up, there was a sign: "Closed from dusk to dawn." It was 10:30 or 11:00 p.m. by that point.

"Don't worry," said Mark, reading my mind. "It's like the 1980s out here. Nobody's going to throw us out."

We drove down a long dirt road to a big parking lot surrounded by shrubbery and trees. There were no streetlights and there was no moon that night, but the sky was full of stars. I had no idea what to expect. Mark took my hand and led me about fifty feet through the darkness. If I were doing this with any other guy I'd just met, I probably would have started worrying that I was with a serial killer, but all I felt was excitement.

I heard the water before I could see it. Then Mark squeezed my hand, and we were there—standing some eighty feet above the shore on the edge of a rocky cliff, the heavens above us and the white caps crashing below us. It was the kind of cliff a character in a film might leap from dramatically. And because there was no artificial light, the Milky Way looked so clear and close in the sky that I felt as though I could reach out and grab it. Mark could see the awe on my face, and he smiled.

"I know," he said. "Pretty spectacular."

When we held hands, I noticed his strong forearms and realized how safe I felt with him. I never wanted to let go, and I sensed that he didn't either. This feeling was something I'd never experienced before.

By the time we got back to the boat, we already had a pretty heavy flirtation going on, but I'd already decided that I was sleeping alone in my room that night. Just like before we met, I didn't feel any pressure to rush anything. Still, I put on my cute burgundy nightgown from Anthropologie. Instead of putting on a show, though, I stuck to my normal nighttime routine: washed my face, brushed my teeth, put lotion on my legs. I posed in the doorway of my bedroom to say good night and gave Mark a kiss on the cheek.

"Thank you for an amazing night," I said softly.

Mark looked me up and down and gently traced the outline of my shoulder with his fingers.

"Good night, Geri," he said.

The next morning, I learned that Mark was right when he said nothing beats waking up on the water—especially because I woke up to a hot cup of Mark's Jamaican coffee, some of the best coffee in the world. We took our mugs to the cockpit.

I looked out at the water and the sky and the sailboats and yachts and ducks gliding by. Gulls flew overhead and occasionally dove into the sea and then emerged with their morning catches. It was all so beautiful that it reminded me of Venice. So, I told Mark about Italy, and I told him about the watchtower. I told him about Stan and Paige and Rebecca, and I told him about working in the Garment District and so much more. One story led to another. He listened, mesmerized, refilling our coffee mugs and making sure I was comfortable. The way he did everything was so effortless and graceful. Mark didn't talk much about his past, except to say that he'd spent a lot of time on his own thinking about how he wanted to move forward in his life.

"I just want to hear you talk," he said. Nearly the whole time, he was spinning his finger around in a circle in my palm. It felt like we were the only two people in the world.

The hours slipped away. I stopped telling my stories when I got to the part about moving back to New York from Boston. I didn't want to bring darkness to the day by giving voice to my sadness about the hysterectomy, the two pregnancies, and the knowledge that I would never bear children.

But then I looked into his eyes and saw nothing but empathy, and I found myself trusting him. The trust was real and ready, and I felt so safe in that moment that I simply told him. I told him everything, and a wave of peace came over me as I spoke. It was cathartic and liberating. His eyes filled with tenderness, but he didn't try to comfort me. He simply listened, and I knew that he truly heard me. We had a mutual empathy that felt like the rarest of gem stones—pure, tangible, and strikingly beautiful.

* * *

Eventually, hunger forced us to get up for a bite to eat. Then, we got on our bikes. Mark had been thrilled when he found out I was an avid cyclist, as bicycles were the easiest way to get around Montauk, so I came prepared with my Trek. Still, he wasn't prepared for just how skilled I was on my bike. Like me, he'd been riding all summer—but he still wasn't quite up to my speed. (Though he was close!) Plus, he was used to riding without baggage, and now he had twenty pounds of beach towels and other supplies strapped to his bike rack. But while some men might have allowed their pride to be wounded by a woman leading the way, Mark got a huge kick out of my prowess.

"You took off like a locomotive!" he said when we got to the beach. "I'm going to have to step it up a notch!"

I just laughed. As far as I was concerned, Mark's physical stamina was a perfect match for my own. At Ditch Plains Beach, we played and swam in the waves together like a couple of seals, breaking through the foam to plant salty kisses on each other under the sun. We were just as playful, if not more playful, than the kids splashing and making castles around us. I could swear we gave off a golden glow. People around us were starting to do double takes, perfect strangers saying things like, "Wow, you guys have great energy!" It was as though whatever we had going on was contagious.

Back at the boat that afternoon, after hours of sun and sand and exercise, Mark and I put our feet up. We were content just to be in each other's presence. I'd brought my new Kindle along, and from time to time I would read aloud to him from the very first book that I downloaded, *The Rosie Project* by Graeme Simsion, a hilarious novel about a socially challenged professor's quest to find the perfect wife. There was something so fitting and poignant about sharing these passages about a romantic quest in the middle of our own romantic quest. I found myself getting attached to the sound of Mark's laugh.

Over dinner that night at Salivar's, a seafood and burger restaurant in town, I had to bring something up to Mark.

"I hope you don't mind," I said, "but I'd like to go to mass tomorrow morning. I usually go on Saturday nights with my parents."

"Of course," said Mark. "There's a Catholic church nearby. I'll look up the mass schedule. Let me just look up the name."

Mark did a quick search on his phone. The name of the church? Saint Thérèse of Lisieux. I should have known!

"I might not go with you," Mark said, a little hesitantly. "Is that okay?"

"Of course," I said, and I meant it. Mark had been raised Catholic, he told me, but he and his brother had never made their confirmations. (Like many teenagers, Mark felt like he had better things to do than go to religious education class.) I knew that Mark was in tune with some kind of higher power, and that was all that mattered to me. What I didn't know at the time was that Mark wasn't going to mass because he wanted some time alone to call his father and talk about me. Mark was in a bit of a pickle, it turned out. Long before I ever made it out to Montauk, he'd invited a woman he'd formerly dated to meet him on the boat later that week. But now that he'd met me, he had no interest in seeing anyone else. He wanted to get his father's opinion on how to handle the situation.

Marked dropped me off at Saint Thérèse on Sunday morning. It was a charming church dating to the 1930s, and it shone bright white against the impossibly blue sky. My head bowed in prayer, I felt overwhelmed with joy. I felt blessed and grateful to God, to Saint Thérèse, and to my grandma Rosaria. I always pray for my grandmother, and I'd just heard a couple of women talking about staying after mass to pray the rosary. My grandma was born in October, the month of the rosary, and was named Rosaria for that reason. I thought of my prayer at the statue of Our Lady of Fatima. I had prayed for someone to love me, but if I were to remain single, I wished to be peaceful and enjoy singlehood.

Could all the signs I was seeing really be coincidences, I wondered? The roses in my hotel room, Mark's finger circling my palm, the name of this church . . . even the fact that the book I was reading happened to be called *The Rosie Project*? I had to keep convincing myself that everything happening to me was real.

When I came out of the church, Mark was waiting for me. He looked so sweet and somehow vulnerable with his youthful physique, his jeans rolled up from walking on the beach, his shirt open at the collar, and his flip-flops in one hand. He smiled as I approached, and I said another silent prayer of thanks. I couldn't believe how lucky I was to have this man waiting for me, waiting to take me out for another magnificent day of sightseeing, sushi, and sunset.

By midnight or so, after hours of riding bikes and playing together in the surf like a couple of teenagers, I'd fallen for him so hard that I didn't want to say goodbye. So, at Mark's urging, I decided to take the next day off from work, too—and I decided to sleep in Mark's bed that night. Lying next to him, I felt tears welling up. I closed my eyes, and Mark began very gently running his fingertips across my face, and neck, and shoulders, and then my entire body. Slowly I felt myself falling into a sort of trance. It was as if suddenly, after years of pushing myself, my body realized it was safe to rest; it was safe to stop and just *be*.

I opened my eyes and looked at him. "I can't tell anyone about you," I said softly. "Because if I let the word out, women will come hundreds of miles just to have coffee with you."

Mark laughed. His touch grounded me and gave me a sense of utter calm. Between the soft rocking of the boat and the rhythm of Mark's breathing, I slept that night like I hadn't in years.

The next morning in the galley, Mark set down his mug of Jamaican coffee.

"Geri," he said, "I have something to ask you."

I froze, and the old panic kicked in. I knew this was too good to be true, I thought. He was going to ask me if I was okay with keeping things casual, now that I'd gone and let myself fall for him.

Mark took my hand with a serious look on his face. "Can we see each other exclusively?" he asked.

I was so relieved that I burst out crying. Before long, tears were running down Mark's face, too. "Mark, if we're going to do this, then I'm going to be *all in*."

I'd always advised people to have courage to be vulnerable, because when one is vulnerable, changes can happen. Mark didn't need my advice: he was strong enough to be completely open. "I know what I want, Geri. I've been looking for you for a long time."

Then Mark told me about the other woman who was supposed to come and visit him and how he'd called his father to ask for his advice. His father had advised him against telling me what was going on. ("You're not going to be an idiot and be honest with her, are you?" were his exact words.)

"But I am going to be honest with you," Mark said, "because I want to be with you, and if this goes somewhere, all of these little choices I make now are going to mean something someday." Then he laughed. "My dad said you'd better be worth it, and I told him, 'Wait till you see her legs, Dad!'"

Chapter Sixteen

Under the Montauk Moon

Even though it was only our third morning together, Mark and I had already settled into a routine: bikes, breakfast, beach. Mark knew all the hidden nooks and crannies of Montauk, so it was a pleasure to follow his lead, even though I was often technically in front (unless we were going up a hill, when Mark's strength gave him a slight advantage). Speeding along Montauk Highway for a breakfast of Triple Delight Eggs Benedict at a place called Bird on a Roof, which has a charming little gift shop that sells beachwear—the cutest little *schmatta*! I luxuriated in the feeling the sun on my skin and the wind in my hair.

I'd pulled farther ahead of Mark than I planned, though, so I did a U-turn on a little side street lined with bright wildflowers to give him time to catch up. But when I got back to the highway, he was nowhere to be seen. I looked down the road in both directions, but there was no trace of him—and not knowing if he was behind me or in front of me, I was afraid to ride too far either way. My heart started pounding. Where could he possibly have gone? Immediately, my mind went to the worst possible scenario. What if he'd gone into cardiac arrest? I remembered that he'd been complaining about a pain in his neck . . . what if it was his carotid artery? I'd finally found the man of my dreams, and now he was probably lying in the shrubbery dying of a heart attack and I couldn't even find him! I didn't have a phone on me; I barely knew where I was. How could I call for help?

Then my mind jumped to another horrible scenario: maybe I'd been ditched. Ditched on the way to Ditch Plains Beach! Maybe everything Mark had said and done so far had all been a lie. Maybe he was a sociopath! As I pedaled my bike in wide circles, hoping to catch a glimpse of Mark but not wanting to stray too far, my mind was going in circles, too. I didn't really believe that Mark was a sociopath, but I just couldn't help feeling like things had been so good, there had to be a catch. This kind of bliss couldn't be real, could it? Thinking that something happened to Mark, I was overcome with sorrow. I'd lost so many people in my life, but I'd never had a feeling like this one before. I finally had everything I ever wanted, and then it was gone. I must really be in love, I thought.

After about ten minutes of desperation (which might not sound like very long, but it is when you're stranded on the side of the road and don't know why), a police officer came driving out of a gravel road leading to the state park. He pulled over next to me.

"Are you okay?" he asked. It must have been obvious that I wasn't. Right away, I started sobbing and shaking.

"I can't find my boyfriend!" I gasped. It was the first time I'd called Mark my boyfriend—the word just slipped out of my mouth. After the conversation we'd had that morning, he *was* my boyfriend, I realized. Mark was my boyfriend!

"He was behind me, and then he was gone," I said. "I don't know where he could be. I think something must have happened to him!"

"Don't worry, we'll find him," the police officer said kindly. He was a young man, and he probably felt bad for me, a fifty-year-old woman on her bike alone, crying about her boyfriend. Then, suddenly, Mark appeared down the road, pedaling toward us.

"Oh my gosh, there he is!" I started crying harder.

"You have a good day, ma'am," the officer said. He was probably glad to have me off his hands!

Mark had biked all the way to town, assuming I was so far ahead that I was out of sight. I can honestly say that I've never been so happy to see anyone in all my life. I was back to bliss, only now I appreciated it even more than before (if that was possible). I was so happy to be by his side that I stayed until 4:00 a.m., even though I had to work that day. Before I left, I wrote him a little message on a business card and left it where he would see when he woke up in the morning:

> *Words cannot express the way I feel*
> *when I'm with you, so I guess I'll*
> *have to tell you next time I see you.*

I saw him very soon—that Thursday night. I had reservations at first about taking another day off from work when I was already working a short week, but my friend Susan Garofalo helped me to make the decision.

She and I were working together on a promotion video for the Y. We'd gotten close in the process, and when I got back to the office, the first thing I did was fill her in on my weekend.

"Geri, he sounds amazing," she said. "And you're absolutely glowing! I've never seen anything like it!"

She was right. For some reason, I was turning more heads than usual, even though I was probably putting less effort into my appearance. It seemed like everything came easier, even finding something to wear. Everything just worked.

Susan convinced me that I should take Friday off and go back to Montauk that Thursday night as Mark wanted me to. "Listen, Geri, think of this time off as a gift. Enjoy it. Use it!"

It was exactly what I needed to hear. For so many years, I'd been programmed to sacrifice everything for work. Work was always my top priority. Now, even though I was still focused when I was at my job, it wasn't my primary focus. My identity was switching gears, which felt surreal. I never expected this to happen, not even when I pictured myself getting married. I remembered Joe George again in that moment, and how he said that I would be receiving a "gift." Was this gift of time off from Grandma Rosaria?

Whenever I had a moment to myself, I would exchange flirty texts with Mark. As much as I wanted to be with him every second, I had to admit that being forced to wait only made my feelings for him more intense. I couldn't wait to get back out to Montauk. I bought a new beach dress for the occasion, heather gray and pale pink—great colors for showing off a tan—with a little slit up the side.

Thursday evening, after my three-and-a-half-hour trek to Montauk in stop-and-go traffic, I walked down the dock to the boat in my flip-flops, breathing the salt air in deeply and exhaling slowly. There was none of the anxiety I usually felt at the start of a new relationship, just total excitement. When Mark took me in his arms, nothing else mattered. We danced to the Ed Sheeran song, "Thinking Out Loud," and the words brought us both to tears.

Mark, of course, had a carefully planned itinerary for our second weekend together. It was like I was in a relationship with Montauk's most charming tour guide. Mark knew exactly which beach to go to for the best sunset at exactly what time, depending on the clouds in the sky. He could tell from the direction of the wind where the waves would be just right for swimming. Every meal we ate was exceptional. Mark knew all the locals, and everywhere we went he was met with smiles and handshakes. But the truth is, I would have been happy doing anything with Mark, anywhere.

He surprised me one day with a short voyage. We took the boat for an overnighter at Sag Harbor, a favorite spot of his family when he was a child. Sag Harbor is around the South Fork peninsula from Montauk. Captain Ken Deeg, the owner of Sag Harbor Moorings, reserved a mooring for us, and when we arrived, we put on our bathing suits and jumped off the swim platform into the warm, August waters of Long Island Sound. Mark turned on the boat's sound system, and I did water aerobics to disco and classic Motown tunes.

Later, he arranged for Captain Ken to pick us up in his water taxi. He and Mark loaded our bikes and beach gear on to the launch, and Captain Ken took us seven miles to the South Ferry, which we hopped aboard for the five-minute ride to Shelter Island.

The island was unbelievably quiet and peaceful. We biked to the Chequit Inn for a farm-to-table lunch and a glass of prosecco. Then we biked around the island, stopping at Sunset Beach for a long swim. On the way back to the ferry, we stopped at a farm stand for tomatoes, lettuce, berries, and sunflowers, which Mark used his MacGyver skills to fasten to the back of his bike. I watched him, impressed, and I knew that I would remember this day forever.

Back on the boat, we relaxed with chilled tequila and a game of backgammon. Then, a nap, a shower, and it was time for dinner. I wore a pastel cotton sundress and a touch of lip gloss, and I pulled my wet hair back with a clip. Mark put on tailored white shorts and a crisp, turquoise, linen shirt, open at the collar. Arm in arm, I strolled with my beautiful man to the American Hotel on Main Street, where the maître d', Richard, greeted us with a smile and glasses of champagne. It was the stuff of dreams, and it felt so *right*.

* * *

Under almost any other circumstances, the idea of introducing my new boyfriend to my parents so soon might have seemed bizarre. But these circumstances were unlike any other. So, I called my mother and invited her and my father to come and meet us in nearby Amagansett. "Trust me, you've really got to meet this guy," I said.

Mom must have heard in my voice that this time was different, so she called to my father, "Richie, let's go! We're going to the beach to meet Geraldine's new friend!"

Their visit started out as a comedy of errors. The plan was to meet for breakfast after they arrived, but since Mark and I got to Amagansett first by bike, we figured we'd surprise them and meet them at the hotel. My parents had arrived earlier than expected, too, and had a similar idea—to surprise us at the restaurant. Once we figured out the mix-up, we told my parents to go ahead and eat without us for the sake of my mother's low blood sugar and to meet us at the beach in front of their hotel.

I remember the sound our bikes made as Mark and I rode over the little wooden bridge leading to the beach, we sounded like a train on the tracks. As soon as the ocean came into view, we both stopped short. It was one of the most stunning sights I'd ever seen—a seemingly endless stretch of soft sand dotted with sunny yellow umbrellas, a blindingly bright-blue sky, and an ocean that danced and glittered like diamonds. The beach should have been packed on a day that perfect, but all the beach chairs were empty.

Mark held up a towel while I changed into my red bikini—and that felt familiar, as though we were little kids. I put my hair into pigtails, then Mark and I ran the hundred yards or so to the water. We dove in and swam out past the breakers to float arm in arm. The waves rolled softly, picking us up ever so gently and setting us back down. It was like we'd been teleported to a place where time stood still.

We settled in with our towels to dry off and wait for my parents. And then, there they were, standing at the top of the beach—my mother with her loose, flowing summer clothes and short black hair, and my father with his Paul Newman eyes. My mother gave Mark a kiss right away and told him that he looked just like her brother Jerry. My father shook Mark's hand and smiled. I took a mental picture. I knew I would want to remember the moment forever.

We needed to bring another umbrella down closer to the water, where we'd set up four chairs. I noticed after a few minutes of walking that my father, who has chronic obstructive pulmonary disease, was struggling to keep up. Mark noticed, too, and immediately offered to help, but my father wouldn't let him. Mark didn't push it, recognizing that my father's refusal was a matter of pride. I wasn't surprised to see Mark handle the situation with such sensitivity, but it warmed my heart just the same.

Once we settled in, my mother started talking, her favorite activity. She asked Mark about his family and told him about ours, especially my Uncle Jerry.

"You're so handsome," she said. "Just like my brother. He has blond hair just like you!"

I didn't bother pointing out that Mark's hair was actually gray. I just smiled.

"Oh, and you're at IBM too, just like Jerry!" she said.

My mother was making connections, linking our families together in her head as if she knew they were destined to come together. I was learning things about Mark from the conversation, too. We knew each other well on a deep level, but there were still so many little details we didn't know. And there were many, many parallels. I knew that Mark and I both had brothers named Christopher, but it wasn't until that morning that I found out that Mark's brother also has a son named Christopher, and like my brother, his name was Christopher Joseph.

Like my parents, Mark's mother and father were fifteen months apart in age. And like my parents, Mark's had never divorced. They were all about the same age. I could tell that my parents were relaxed and having a good time, which put me even more at ease.

After a while, though, I was getting hot. "Come on, Mark, let's go back in the water," I said.

I jumped up and ran toward the water. As I was running, my father must have gotten a paternal premonition because he said, "Uh-oh," and just then, I tripped, my foot slipping into a hole in the sand. Even though it hurt, I couldn't help laughing. It was like I was a little kid again and I was showing off in front of my parents and not caring what anyone thought.

My folks had eaten breakfast, but Mark and I were starving, so we made plans to meet them later at the hotel, and we hopped on our bikes and rode to Cyril's Fish House. The owner, Cyril, was well known for being a character, and he lived up to the hype. About five feet tall with a gray beard and a round belly, Cyril was from Ireland and had a thick brogue. Mark went up to say hello as we were leaving and to praise his amazing shrimp salad and local produce. I introduced myself.

"I'm part Irish, too," I said. "My last name is Brown."

"You're a mix," said Cyril decisively.

"I do have some English," I said, "and my mother's family is Italian."

"A mix," Cyril said.

Mark thought that was the funniest thing. He kept reminding me the rest of the day that I was a "mix" as far as Cyril was concerned. Later, he told me that I wasn't a mix at all, as far as he was concerned; I was all heart, and he loved that about me.

We made it back to the hotel in time for my father's traditional 3:00 p.m. gin martini. It was happy hour, as he called it. He made gin and tonics for the rest of us, too, and we all sat together and drank them on the beach. My mom is a talker like me, and my dad is a man of few words. But Mark had a way of getting Dad to share stories. As he talked, Mom and I found ourselves looking at each other as if to say, "I didn't know that!"

Sitting on the beach in the Hamptons that afternoon, I thought how different it felt from the last time I'd been there. It was Halloween weekend the previous year, and I'd gone alone to the spa at Gurney's to decompress from another stressful grand opening and to contemplate life during solitary walks on the empty beach. It was cold, but I was grateful that the sky was clear—fourteen inches of snow was falling in Scarsdale that weekend. Now I was sitting in the same place, but my life was totally different . . . in the best way possible.

Things were simply falling into place effortlessly. That synchronicity was exemplified by our serendipitous encounter with Myrna and Elliott, a couple who joined my parents and Mark and me for tapas later that day. Mark and I had met them one day while having sushi at the bar at Salivar's. Myrna had an outgoing bohemian elegance, and Elliott, it turned out, was involved in mall development. He was working on a project in Scarsdale, of all places. We chatted before they were seated at a table for lunch, and then we went back to our sushi and our discussion of how we'd spend my visit.

Mark had asked me to list the top three things I wanted to do in Montauk, and the first thing I said was go fishing. I loved to fish—I'd even traveled to Mexico for the fishing. As we were leaving Salivar's that day, we stopped at Elliott and Myrna's table to say good-bye. Out of the blue, Elliott said that he'd booked a deep-sea fishing excursion, and someone in his party had just dropped out; would we like to join him?

I realized at dinner that night at Swallow East that my relationship with my mother was also changing since I met Mark. Since I'd done so much eating out at restaurants for work over the years, it had become the custom in our family for me to order for everyone, or at least help the process along. Without even noticing it, I'd fallen into a similar pattern with Mark: if he didn't have a preference about what to eat or couldn't make up his mind, I'd go ahead and choose for him. It wasn't something I ever really thought about, but my mother had apparently come to rely on my recommendations. When all six of us went out for tapas later, my first instinct when we sat down at our table was to help Mark with the menu. (Actually, he didn't have his glasses, so I didn't really have a choice!) I'd barely glanced at the wine list when my mother interrupted me.

"Geraldine, what are we having?"

"Hang on a second. I'm just helping Mark," I said. "Why don't you take a look, see what looks good?"

I went back to the menu, but again, a minute or two later, Mom said, "Geraldine, what are we having?"

"I don't know yet. Hang on," I said. Why wouldn't she stop pestering me? Eventually, I put her off so many times that she gave up and turned to my father for help. It didn't occur to me until later, when Mark and I were rehashing the evening, what was really going on. It was simple, really. My mother was used to getting my attention, and now I was giving that attention to Mark. It was a subtle shift, but a significant one, because it proved that my mother was picking up on the strength of my bond with Mark. She was sensing that for the first time in my life, I might actually belong to someone else besides my father and her.

I did feel like I belonged to Mark already, even though we'd only known each other for a few weeks. But it was the next week that our union truly solidified in a physical sense. Though we'd slept in the same bed and been intimate on so many levels, we were still taking things slow sexually. Just as with every other aspect of our relationship, we didn't feel any need to rush that side of things. Of course, we were still extremely attracted to each other, and waiting only made those feelings more intense.

On Labor Day weekend, we spent Saturday sunbathing on the bow of the boat, sipping George Clooney's Casamigos tequila, listening to music, and dancing. Mark was shirtless and tanned and flirtatious and *so* handsome. When I got too hot, he sprinkled water from his bottle over my back. Other boaters nearby probably thought we were acting like teenagers; from time to time, we felt curious eyes on us, but we were too euphoric to care.

Sleepy from the sun and the tequila, we decided to recharge with a Montauk nap and then go out to explore the nightlife. We started at Lynn's Hula Hut/Tiki Bar and then went to the yacht club. After dinner, we stopped at Liar's Saloon, an iconic tavern next to the marina that attracted everyone from local fishermen to Wall Street types, to check out the scene and dance. Liar's has a late "last call," and the place was full of twenty-somethings that night. As usual, our vibe attracted attention and conversation. It was as if we were shouting to the younger clientele, "Look what you have to look forward to!" One young man christened Mark "the Silver Fox."

We went back to the boat and fell asleep with our heads directly under the hatch, the opposite direction from the way we usually slept. It must have been close to midnight when something suddenly made me open my eyes.

"Oh my God," I said aloud. I was looking up through

the hatch at the fullest moon anyone could ever imagine. It was the kind of view you'd expect to see out the window of a space shuttle, not a boat. Mark's eyes blinked open.

The second he caught sight of that moon, Mark jumped out of bed and started getting dressed. "Come on," he said. "Let's go!"

"What are we doing?" I asked him, pulling my hair into a ponytail.

"Wait until you see," he said mysteriously.

Within minutes, we were in the car, wearing our matching red fleeces, and heading toward Camp Hero. This time, instead of going out on the bluffs, Mark took me down a long, gravel road to the water's edge.

Excitement heightened my senses. I heard the sounds of summer around us, smelled sea salt in the air, felt the warmth of Mark's arm linked through mine. We stopped often to kiss, so it took us a while to get there. But when we finally did, it was yet another magnificent Montauk reveal. The moonlight gave everything a luminous, otherworldly quality, bathing the waves and the ancient-looking rock formations in a silvery glow. Mark took my hand, and we walked out on a smooth rock buffeted by the swirling foam.

We felt truly and deeply in love in that moment. We were both adults with years of relationships behind us, but there in the moonlight, it felt as if we were starting something entirely new, something different than either of us had ever experienced. His touch on my skin was sublime. We fit perfectly, like hand in glove. Exposed to the elements and exposed to each other. Afterward,

Mark held me with his arms wrapped around me from behind. He was holding my shoulders back, so my chest—like my heart—was open. We watched the waves roll out to the horizon for hours until the faintest glow appeared in the east. It wasn't until we spotted two fisherman surf casting in their waders that we felt any desire to leave.

Later, Mark told me about going to Camp Hero by himself a few days before we first got in touch. He'd just been spending time alone, he said, making sure that he was clear with his past and content and ready for the future. He took a long bike ride out to the bluffs the morning of the night we met, and as he sat looking out at the water, he was overcome with a feeling of peace.

"That's when I offered up a little prayer to my grandparents who'd passed away," he told me.

"I just did a little shout-out to them. I said, 'You know, guys, I'm doing great, but I could use a little help.'"

Like me, Mark had found a way to accept being alone. But he didn't really believe that the single life was his fate. Also like me, he was more than ready to meet his destiny and eager for Heaven's help in finding it.

Chapter Seventeen

Coming Up Roses

Over all my years of witnessing my friends finding their soul mates, I'd noticed that this change in their lives often resulted in physical transformation, too. Sometimes it would be tangible, like a significant weight loss; Mark had been steadily dropping pounds since we'd gotten together, even though he was in good shape to begin with. Other times, though, it was harder to define, though no less noticeable. People call it a "glow," and I believe that's because what we're seeing when someone is in love is a visible shift in his or her energy. That's what was happening to me. When Mark and I were together, everywhere we went people commented on our good vibes and how beautiful we looked together—how in love.

Even when we were apart, I was getting comments left and right. One of the regulars at the YMCA, a seventy-year-old Russian Jewish woman named Reni who never missed an aerobic swim class gave me the nickname Yaffa, which meant "beautiful from the inside out."

"You're like a flower that's blossomed," she told me.

It was true that I was getting the attention of a lot

of honeybees! Not that Mark had anything to worry about. When I said I was "all in" on the boat, I meant it. And I knew he meant it too. But behind the excitement of this new love unfolding, there was also a fear about how we would keep things going once the season was over. Mark had been living on the boat all summer and had spent the previous winter in the Clinton, Connecticut, home of his friends Sean and Lori, who had bought a second home in Florida. I still had my one-bedroom apartment in Scarsdale. We were ready to start a life together; we just weren't sure where to do it. Mark even offered to get rid of the boat, but I wouldn't hear of it. That would have been like stripping the hair off his chest.

Eventually, we decided that Mark would move in with me in Scarsdale, and we'd make it work until then as we tied up all the loose ends of our lives.

Not long after we made that decision, we went to Sean and Lori's house in Clinton for a small get-together. The house was right across the street from a marina, and it had high ceilings, original Dali artwork on the walls, sunflowers decorating the upstairs rooms, and a widow's walk overlooking Long Island Sound. One thing I noticed the second I entered the door was the compass rose—a circle showing north, south, east, and west—inlaid in the wood floor. I felt a shudder as I stepped in, as if I were stepping on my true north. I absolutely loved the house at first sight.

I liked Sean and Lori right away, too. They'd been very close to Mark for a few years and had seen him through his divorce. Slowly, I'd been learning more about Mark's separation from his wife and what he'd been through, and I understood why, like me, he'd needed to spend time alone for a while before he was ready to move on. Like most failed relationships, Mark and his ex-wife's involved a lot of hurt and confusion. But there had been an extra element of tragedy. Mark and his ex had run a horse farm together, back when Mark was more focused on motorcycles than on boats. The final nail in the coffin of their marriage had been the death of his wife's beloved horse from Cushing's disease. Since they didn't have any children together, the horse was like her baby. And as it so often happens when a couple loses a child, the marriage couldn't survive the impact.

Sean and Lori knew exactly where Mark had been and where he wanted to go, and they liked me because they knew I was the right partner for his journey. After observing us together at the party that night, they were so inspired and touched by what we had that they made an unbelievable offer.

"Why don't you two take the house when we go back to Florida for the winter?" Sean asked Mark as they sat on the front porch smoking cigars and drinking Scotch.

It was a perfect fit for us. Mark would be able to continue working at IBM, and the boat could stay across the street at the dock. I would eventually have to leave the Y, but I was ready for a change of direction in my career, anyway. I wanted to help people. Now that I'd been blessed with this sense of peace and direction, I wanted to bring that feeling to other people. I wanted people to know that it was never too late to find love.

And every time I started to wonder if I was living in a fantasy, I'd get some little sign of confirmation. Everywhere I turned, I saw hearts and roses. It was like the world was turning into one big Valentine. Roses in graffiti, heart-shaped rocks on the ground, and hearts in the wood grain of a tabletop. Even a bleach stain on my sweater was in the shape of a heart.

There was no question that we would get married. There wasn't a question of when, either. We knew we wanted to get married in August, one year after we met. But Mark wanted to surprise me with an official proposal. He wanted to surprise me with a ring, too, but unlike most brides-to-be, I didn't care about that.

"Mark, save your money," I said. "Flashy rings are for young girls. All I want is to make the sacrament of marriage and have a band around my finger that shows everybody I belong to you."

I really meant it. I wasn't attached to the idea of a diamond ring at all. I'd had one on my finger years before, with Ray, and I'd been miserable. So, I knew that a ring in and of itself was meaningless.

Not to Mark, it would turn out. One night, we were out to dinner at a favorite restaurant, Harvest on Hudson in Hastings on Hudson, New York. The patio was surrounded by vegetable and flower gardens and couldn't have been more romantic, and we were in our typical cloud of love-induced endorphins. Angelo, one of the principals, came over when he saw us and gave us each a big hug. The Harvest, as we called it, had been my favorite restaurant for fifteen years. Angelo and Kevin, the bartender, and other staff members were like family to me. They'd lived my singlehood with me, treating me like gold when I'd come in, exhausted from a business trip, and just wanted to sit with a book and enjoy a fine meal. They'd given the thumbs up or thumbs down to many of my dates over the years. When Angelo met Mark, though, he said all bets were off. Mark was the one. Now, Angelo congratulated us on our engagement and bought us drinks.

Mark and I always sat at the bar for dinner because the bartender, Kevin, was such a great conversationalist and host. We'd just gotten settled when a friend I hadn't seen in a while spotted us and came over. I introduced her to Mark and broke our big news. As soon as she heard, she grabbed my hand. "Where's your ring?" she asked.

I just brushed it off and laughed, but I could tell the question bugged Mark. He didn't say anything about it right away, and I forgot about it. Then a few days later, he woke up with a question for me. "So, if I did get you a ring, what kind would you want?"

"Mark!" I rolled my eyes. "How many times have we been over this? I don't need a ring! Save your money. Put it into the boat!"

He dropped it for the moment, but over the next days and weeks, he kept bringing it up. I couldn't understand why. The thing I was forgetting to factor into the equation, of course, was the male ego. To have a fiancée with a bare ring finger made Mark look bad, or at least that's how he felt. But at the time, I thought it was an unjustifiable expense.

One thing I *could* justify spending money on,

however, was a sale at Lord & Taylor. On my way out the door one Sunday morning to pick up some Clarins makeup I'd ordered during a charity promotion presale, I asked Mark if he wanted to come along—not because I expected it to be an exciting errand, but because, as cheesy as it sounds, having Mark with me just made everything more fun. While plenty of other men might have politely (or not so politely) declined an invitation to go makeup shopping at a department store, Mark was game.

We were both in good moods when we got there and not in any rush. As we walked toward the makeup area, Mark saw me looking at clothing displays, and he did what he sometimes does to keep me from being distracted. Laughing, he held his hand up in front of us and said, "Follow the hand."

Then he spotted the jewelry counter. "Hey, let's take a look," he said. "Just for fun."

He'd brought up the subject of a ring again that morning, and again, I'd said, "I don't want a ring. This is about us, not a ring." But I followed the hand to the jewelry counter, not even thinking about an engagement ring, since Lord & Taylor's isn't really the kind of store where people generally go for that kind of purchase.

Literally, the very first thing we saw in the case was a gorgeous, white-gold ring with three tiers of three baguettes. It was resting on black velvet, and the diamonds sparkled as if Tinker Bell had spread fairy dust on them. The ring was practically glowing.

Mark and I both put our hands on the glass, my left

and his right, so that our fingers were touching over that ring. I'd never seen anything like it. As we looked at it, a hand slid into the display case from the back and picked it up. I looked up to see a round little saleswoman, probably about five foot two, with a warm smile and kind eyes. Without saying a word, she slid the ring onto my finger.

It fit perfectly, as though it had been made for me, and I became overwhelmed with emotion.

"Look," I whispered, pointing to the three tiers of diamonds. "It's the Holy Trinity—the Father, the Son, and the Holy Ghost."

"I've never seen anything like it here before," the saleswoman said. "It looks beautiful on you." Her Italian accent made me look at her again. Her nametag, I now noticed, said *Rosaria*.

"You share my grandmother's name!" I said, my heart racing. "You don't go by Rose or Rosie?"

"No," she said. "I am Rosaria."

Immediately, my thoughts went to Joe George and what he had told me in the airport years earlier. *Your grandmother has a message for you.* The blood pounding in my ears blocked out all other sound, and I needed to walk away to collect myself. I murmured to Mark that I'd be back in a moment and found myself moving toward the makeup counter, my grandmother's face flashing in my mind. Was this her way of telling me that Mark was the one, or maybe even that she'd been instrumental in bringing us together?

The young saleswoman behind the makeup counter looked concerned when she saw me. "Miss," she asked, "are you all right?"

"Something's happening to me," I said as tears spilled down my cheeks. "I've never ever felt this way before in my life."

But I had felt that way once before, I realized—on the day of my First Holy Communion. Was this feeling what people call grace? I wondered. I'd never really understood the meaning of grace, even though I'd spent my entire life praying for it and searching for it.

The young saleswoman handed me a tissue, and as I gratefully dabbed at my cheeks, I looked at her—really looked at her. She was about thirty and had the kindest eyes. "You're so beautiful," I told her. "What's your name?"

"Thank you," she said, smiling. "My name is Grace."

My mouth opened, but I couldn't speak. This was completely surreal. I walked back to the jewelry counter in a daze, not even feeling my legs moving or my feet on the floor.

Mark and Rosaria were still talking. "It's strange we even have this ring," Rosaria was saying. "We seldom get diamond rings, and never this kind." She looked up at me. "It's beautiful, just like the two of you."

"Thank you very much," I said, feeling somewhat grounded again, now that I was standing next to Mark.

"You know," Rosaria said, "my son-in-law, he bought my daughter a $35,000 engagement ring. And she doesn't wear it! It sits in a drawer because she's so afraid to lose it. What a waste! But you," she said, "you will wear this ring."

"Thirty-five thousand dollars!" I said. "What does

your son-in-law do for a living?"

"He owns a bridal shop on Central Avenue in Yonkers," she said. "It's called Amelia's."

Amelia's Bridal Boutique was a famous shop, it turned out, which explained how Rosaria's son-in-law could afford a $35,000 ring.

"Maybe I'll look for my dress there," I said. "Would you mind giving me his number?"

"I don't have his business card with me, but I'll write down his number on my card," Rosaria said. "I just have to find one."

Rosaria handed Mark the box bearing the store logo, and I saw yet another reason why we'd been led to this store: the famous Lord & Taylor logo, a rose. Meanwhile, the saleswoman was pulling out drawers and looking on shelves, searching everywhere for a business card. I was about to tell her she could just write down his number on the receipt when she pulled one out of a box with a triumphant smile. "I got it! I found one!"

She wrote down the names of her daughter Carmela and son-in-law Giovanni on the back of the card and handed it to me. "You tell them I sent you," she said.

"Thank you," I said. "This is perfect." Then I turned the card over. There, printed in black, was my grandmother's name: Rosaria Gentile.

"Mark! Rosaria Gentile!" I said. My hands were shaking so hard I almost dropped the card. "That's my grandmother's name! She was a Gentile before she got married!"

Mark's jaw dropped.

There was no doubt in my mind now that my

grandmother was sending me signs. This was the clearest sign I ever could have hoped for.

I ran around the corner of the counter, ignoring the "Employees Only" sign, and gathered Rosaria into a big hug. I could hear myself screaming, "Oh, my God! Oh my God!" but it was almost as if I was floating outside of my body. Tears were streaming down her face, and Mark was crying too. The other shoppers must have thought we were insane.

This beautiful ring truly *was* meant to be mine, I realized. Then, Grandma Rosaria's message dawned on me, and it was a thousand times more precious: *know what the Little Flower knew*, she was telling me.

Grandma Rosaria had been devoted to Saint Thérèse, the Little Flower, because of Thérèse's absolute conviction that God loved her. Thérèse *knew* that His love existed; she felt it. When those thoughts came together in my mind, the shame I'd been carrying since I'd ended those two pregnancies fell away. In that moment, I suddenly knew that I *was* worthy of the sacrament of marriage after all. I knew that God still loved me. And He would always love me.

Thank you, Grandma. Thank you, thank you, thank you!

* * *

Now that we had a ring, I knew my official proposal was likely coming soon. On March 11, the day before my birthday, we woke up in the morning and Mark suggested we go for a bike ride on the Bronx River

Parkway, something we did often. I was happy to go, but I was in no rush, and I had lots of little weekend chores to get done around the house. But Mark kept nagging me to get going.

"Almost ready?" he asked, standing by the door.

"One sec," I said, a broom still in my hand.

"Now?" he asked a couple of minutes later as I wiped down a countertop.

Finally, he got me on the bike. He took the lead right away, and I had a hard time keeping up with him. It was the opposite of Montauk. "Slow down! What's the hurry?" I yelled as I followed him up a hill.

"I've got a pain in my foot that won't go away until we get to where we're going," he yelled back. "You wouldn't understand!"

When we got to the statue of Our Lady of Fatima, we stopped. Mark took my hand, and we sat down on a bench. It seemed like he was on a mission. He checked the time on his phone, then got down on one knee and started digging in his sock with his finger. I had no idea what was going on until he pulled out the ring—he'd been hiding it in his sneaker the whole ride!

Mark asked me to marry him at 11:11 a.m. on March 11, 2016. Suddenly, I understood why he'd been rushing me out the door that morning. As always, Mark's timing was perfect. He wanted Grandma Rosaria to be part of the moment. He was giving a nod to that long-ago All Saints Day, November 1, on which I'd been given Mother Teresa's boarding pass for a flight that had taken place on November 1. I was beginning to see that this was how destiny worked—or, more accurately, how grace worked.

Shortly after Mark proposed, I decided to go to the noon mass at Sacred Heart Church near the Bronx. I liked the priest there, Father Christian, and the way he chanted like a monk. I went into the confessional to speak to him after mass. "Father," I said, "this is beyond a confession. I don't even know how to explain the way I'm feeling. I'm so happy and filled with love and so grateful that I'm coming out of my skin."

I told Father Christian my story, and he started crying. I'd never heard of a priest crying in a confessional! Naturally, I was crying too, and neither one of us could find a tissue. But we didn't even care. "The reason you're feeling this way," Father Christian told me, "is because you're in a state of grace. I don't know how long it will last, and it will probably ebb and flow, but this is a great gift."

There was that word again: *gift*.

"You know, Father," I said, "back when I was younger and I told my parents I wanted my own family, I just wanted to belong to somebody and something. And now I know that Mark is that person."

"God bless you both," said Father Christian. "Thank you, Geraldine, for sharing this story with me."

Mark and I were meeting more and more special people in each other's lives, but there was one person I needed him to meet sooner rather than later. My dear, dear friend Sister Eileen had been a very important person to me for several years. We met shortly after I quit my job in Boston, when I was doing some freelance consulting and occasionally meeting with a headhunter. I was driving back from an interview in Manhattan for a miserable-sounding job I had no interest in when I decided to pull into the parking lot of the Sisters of Saint Francis Convent. As a middle-aged woman, Grandma Rosaria had been an associate of that order. So, in my mind, it was like maybe she was sending me there, even though I wasn't entirely sure what I was looking for besides some sense of purpose. I knew I didn't want to become a nun; I'd never felt that calling. But there had to be some way I could help.

At first, the nuns who greeted me seemed confused by my desire to get involved, but after they looked at my résumé, they decided I should speak with Sister Eileen, who ran training workshops for catechists. That night, Sister and I spoke on the phone for two hours, gabbing away like old girlfriends. She was thrilled to have someone with real-world experience offering help, no strings attached, and she wasn't shy about using my skills. She invited me to work on various projects and go with her on retreats.

Sister Eileen taught me so many things and helped to focus me during a challenging time of transition just by reminding me to live for compassion and forgiveness. Sister Eileen believed in the power of words, and she made me more conscious of the messages I put out in the world, too.

More than anything else, Sister was simply my friend. She was someone I loved. When I got the job working for Westchester's Ridge Hill shopping center, I saw less of Sister Eileen, but I still thought about her every day. So, when I got the call that her doctor had found a dark spot on her pancreas, my heart broke. Here, I'd found the love of my life, but I was losing my best friend to cancer. I visited Sister in the hospital during my lunch hours, as the hospital was, fortunately, within walking distance of my office. I wanted to bring Mark to meet her, but she kept saying, "When I get better, when I get better."

Soon enough, it became apparent that Sister wasn't going to get better. When I got the call that it was time to say good-bye, Mark got in the car with me to drive to Mount Vernon. My chest hurt thinking about Sister.

"Listen, I'm not sure if you should come in with me at first," I told Mark when we arrived. "I don't know what I'm going to see when I get in there."

"Of course," said Mark.

What I saw made me sad. Sister looked so frail, sitting in her recliner chair with oxygen tubes up her nose.

"Geri, please sit down here with me," she asked. "I can't talk much, but I want to see you."

I held Sister's hand and looked around her apartment, thinking how much I would miss our times together in this place.

"I want you to take something with you to remember me by, Geri," Sister said, following my gaze.

"Come on, really?" My eyes were tearing up. "Sister, you're going to be in my heart forever. I don't need some little tchotchke to remember you!"

"I know what you should have," Sister said. "The photograph your mother gave me for my jubilee party, the one she took of the sunflower."

When Sister said *sunflower*, I remembered Mark.

I'd recently told him that he had sunflower eyes—sea-green-blue with perfect sunflowers in the middle. He'd been waiting outside for a half hour now. "Oh, Sister!" I said. "I left my fiancé in the car. Is it okay if I bring him in?"

"Of course," she said. "Go get him. I want to meet him."

I ran out to the car, carrying the framed sunflower picture.

"Mark, Mark!" I said. "Look! Sunflower eyes!"

Mark came inside with me and sat beside Sister Eileen. He held her hand.

"Mark," she said. "I want you to promise that you'll never leave Geraldine's side."

"I won't, Sister. I promise."

She died two days later.

Chapter Eighteen

Amazing Grace

As someone who'd spent years planning events for work, I was in my element organizing our wedding. I couldn't help but think about when I was engaged to Ray and wedding planning felt like a horrible chore. What a difference the right man makes!

Most wedding venues, florists, and caterers are booked months or even years in advance, and our timeline was so short that I expected some stress. Instead, things just kept falling into place. And my grandmother kept showing up everywhere. Looking through the closet one day, my mother stumbled across a baseball cap I'd sent her from Faneuil Hall. I'd had one of the Marketplace vendors paint *Ring Around the Rosie* on it. To me, the word *ring* represented the circular bond between Grandma Rosaria, Mom, and me.

Not long after that, my cousin Stephanie made an interesting discovery related to Grandma Rosaria. Stephanie, the daughter of my uncle Jerry, was going to be my matron of honor. Unlike some brides, I had no desire to force anyone to wear a dress she hated or didn't feel comfortable in, so I told her to choose one for herself. She found one she loved at Amelia's, where

I was getting my dress. When she got home, she called me right away.

"Geraldine, you're not going to believe this," she said.

Stephanie told me that she'd been thinking about how familiar her dress seemed, and then she found a picture of herself wearing the very same dress in a different color at our cousin's wedding thirty years before.

"I'm going to send you this picture right now," she said. "Grandma Rosaria is in it, too."

A few seconds later, the photo showed up on my phone. There was a young Stephanie wearing the dress, standing next to Grandma Rosaria, who was wearing a pink dress that showed off just a little bit of cleavage. As humble as she was, she was still a woman and had her share of vanity! On my grandmother's chest, I noticed a strange red spot.

"Stephanie, what's that thing on Grandma's chest?" I asked.

"I saw that. I don't know," she said. "It's weird, right? I'm positive it didn't used to be there."

With so much to do, I filed the mystery of the red spot away in my mind and got back to nuptial preparations. Stephanie wasn't the only one who needed a dress. My bear, Emma Jean, needed one too. F.R.O.G. and Emma Jean were to be honored guests at the wedding, and I wanted them to look their best. The agreeable people at Colin's Tuxedos in Old Saybrook, Connecticut, had fitted F.R.O.G. with a little tux (I think they got a kick out of the request), while Emma Jean was dressed by my current babysitting charge, Ella Grace.

When I'd moved to Clinton, I'd needed a break from my usual line of work and some time to consider future options, such as life coaching. I put feelers out for babysitting jobs because I love spending time with kids, and immediately, a woman called me. We hit it off, and I instantly became an aunt to her three children. I even helped train their dog. That job brought me so much joy that I probably would have done it for free. Ella Grace, who was six, was probably more excited than anyone about my wedding. Everywhere I took her, she would tell people about it.

"My babysitter is getting married!" she announced to the ice cream man one day.

Ella Grace loved helping me make decisions for my wedding, and when I mentioned that Emma Jean needed an outfit, she knew just what to do.

"Come with me," she said, leading me to a huge closet in her playroom filled with American Girl clothes. After we picked out the perfect party dress, Ella took Emma Jean upstairs and started to take off her old prairie garb. It was then that I saw the tag on Emma Jean for the first time. The bear had been a "gift with purchase" at Lord & Taylor, of all places. Even crazier, Ella's mom, Michelina, had worked at Lord & Taylor some twenty years earlier and remembered when the bear was being given away as a promotion. When I told Mark, a huge grin filled his face. "Your grandmother is working overtime," he said.

Mark's parents and my parents hadn't even met yet, and Mark still had to make his confirmation after all these years. It wasn't a requirement for us to get married in the church, but Catholics generally make the sacrament of confirmation before marriage, and Mark wanted to take this step as further proof that he was all in.

Mark's mother, Pat, and I clicked right away. We were both born under the sign of Pisces, and we're both creative and left-handed. When I told Pat that Mark and I weren't sure what venue we wanted for the reception, or even what town, she suggested that we take a look at Old Saybrook, Connecticut, a lovely town right on the water and only about ten minutes away from Clinton, where Mark's boat was docked. Several places there would be absolutely perfect for a wedding, she said, including a winery and a museum.

The one thing Mark and I knew we wanted was the date: we wanted to get married on the first Saturday in August, a year after the first weekend we spent together. The only problem was, that wasn't very far away. The first place I called, Water's Edge, was already booked. So, I moved on to my future mother-in-law's next recommendation: Saybrook Point Inn. I spoke with a wedding planner named Valerie, giving her the basic rundown: we'd be having fewer than a hundred guests, we wanted a buffet, and there would be no wedding party, just a matron of honor.

"We just want simple elegance," I told her. "We're a very close family. All you're going to feel is love."

"Sounds beautiful," Valerie said. "And what day were you thinking?"

Saturday, August 6, was already taken. I was about to move on when Valerie asked me if we would consider having the wedding on a Friday instead.

Well . . . Mark and I had actually met on a Friday, I thought. "Why didn't I think of that? I said. "Just give me ten minutes to talk to the church!"

Mark had been so excited after we became engaged that he'd called Saint Mary's in Clinton and reserved the church for Saturday, August 6. So, after checking with Mark to make sure he was okay with the Saybrook Point Inn ("I just have a feeling," I said), I called Saint Mary's. Once again, everything lined up perfectly. It turned out there'd been a conflict with the original time on Saturday, so Friday was better anyway. I told them I wanted to get married at noon, which is one of three times daily when the Angelus prayer is said. Grandma Rosaria would always stop what she was doing at noon and say that prayer, with my mother joining in, and I wanted to honor her that way. Then I called Valerie to confirm. We were ready to roll.

Speaking of rolling, Mark and I also got (almost) matching license plates reading ALLINMTK and A11INMTK. It was a small thing, but I wanted every facet of our lives to be symbolic of the love we had for each other.

I'd gone to Amelia's Bridal Boutique to look at wedding gowns, and when the manager, Rosa, heard my story of meeting Mark and the ring, she said, "Joe George was giving you a reading."

I had tried on a gown by Maggie Sottero, and I loved it. But inexplicably, I'd been gaining weight, even though I was just as active as usual. My neck was getting puffy, and the dress was strapless. So, when Maria, the staff member who helped me into it, said, "Enough with the stories. Are you going to say yes to the dress?"

I had to say maybe. I wanted a second opinion. So, I arranged for my cousin Steph to meet me at Amelia's. On the appointed day, I went into the changing room to put on the dress and asked Rosa to let me know when Steph arrived. When Rosa gave me the signal, I walked out and twirled around.

Steph loved it. "This is all I needed to see," she told me. "You're done!"

Throughout the planning and figuring things out, Mark was right by my side. He sat with me through every single appointment and humored me when I agonized over which wedding favors to choose. I would email him endless revisions of my to-do lists to print out at work, and he would do it without complaint, sending me sweet notes back: "Hi, hon; I printed the copies! Love you with all my heart!" or "See you soon! Foot massage coming your way!" or "We are so blessed!"

We felt those blessings in the most unforgettable way possible on the night of his confirmation. Before church, we had dinner with Mark's parents at Fresh Salt, the Saybrook Point Inn's restaurant. Valerie, the wedding planner, came by our table to say hello. After greeting everyone, she asked if she could steal the bride and groom for a moment. Mark and I followed her to a set of French doors leading to a room that was all set up for someone else's wedding. She wanted our thoughts on some of the decorations.

Mark's eye was drawn to the wedding cake. "Wow, that's a beautiful cake," he said.

Not only did Valerie make sure we got the very same cake, but she gave it to us as a gift. She was a generous person, and like other businesspeople we encountered, she became a part of the magic of our story. But the gift of the cake was nothing compared with the gift we got later, after Mark's confirmation.

Most people make their confirmations when they're about eleven years old, and at church that evening, Mark sat with the kids in his class. It was adorable. Confirmation is the sacrament when Catholics receive the gift of the Holy Spirit, the next step in the spiritual journey after baptism and the Holy Eucharist. It "confirms" (hence the name) our place in the church and gives us the strength and inspiration we need to carry on in our faith. I acted as his sponsor, standing by his side as the bishop gave him his confirmation name: Joseph. Mark had chosen that name to honor his father, Joe, and his Sicilian grandfather, to whom he had prayed to send him a companion.

Mark was still wearing his red confirmation cape after mass was over, and his parents had gone home. We walked down the dock to the boat hand in hand. I felt like I was in the state of grace times twenty. Mark's mother had given us an engagement gift of two hand-blown champagne glasses, and we'd saved them for this very moment. We set up YouTube to play Carrie Underwood singing "How Great Thou Art" on the boat sound system, and we stood face to face under the slowly darkening sky.

"I'm so thankful for you and that you're making these sacraments," I told Mark, my voice catching in my throat. "I'm so happy for you and how your life is going to change now."

Tears were falling from Mark's eyes now, too. The sun was setting with the most unbelievable colors I'd ever seen, almost like a kaleidoscope. As "How Great Thou Art" ended, the sky flashed with lightning, and there was a sudden clap of thunder so loud that the boat shook under our feet like the earth was quaking. Mark and I held each other until it subsided and the strains of "Amazing Grace" filled the air.

We pulled apart and looked at each other.

There was no storm. That lightning had literally come out of the blue. We took it as a beautiful sign from Heaven.

* * *

I would have been content to stay in that place of spiritual bliss with Mark forever, but there were still some wedding details to work out. One was where I'd be staying the night before the wedding. I wanted to stick to the tradition of the groom not seeing the bride before the wedding, so I didn't want to sleep on the boat with Mark. On a whim, I asked Valerie about the "lighthouse room" at the inn. It was three times the rate of a regular room and usually booked a year in advance, but it was so beautiful I figured I might as well ask.

"Oh, my goodness," Valerie said when she checked. "It's actually available!" And, then, saying how touched she was by our story, she gave the room to me as a gift, just as she had the cake. Her generosity left me speechless.

The remaining items on my to-do list seemed to work out almost effortlessly. Finding shoes and earrings was one of them. My mother told me she'd had good luck finding shoes on Zappos, so I looked at the website, but I had some questions. I wasn't expecting miracles when I called the customer service line, but the equivalent of a retail miracle is what I got. The service rep stayed on the phone with me from 9:00 p.m. until midnight, chatting about the perfect accessories for my dress (which was a very subtle champagne color that looked white in photos). I emailed a photo of it to her so she would have a sense of the look I wanted. She found a pair of Badgley Mischka shoes that I adored and earrings for both my matron of honor and me. She also found fun beaded flip-flops we could wear for taking pictures on the beach.

"I have to tell you, I've never had customer service like this in my life," I told her as we wrapped up our call.

"My pleasure," said the woman. "And congratulations!"

A few days later, I got a card in the mail with cut-out pictures of my dress, the shoes, and the earrings, and a lovely note from the Zappos rep. She'd given me the VIP discount on my purchases. I just shook my head in wonder.

That wasn't even the only outstanding customer service experience I had that week. With so much on my mind, I'd accidentally paid my Lord & Taylor bill twice. I called the store's credit service, wanting to make sure the money was back in my account for our honeymoon. I explained my mistake to the woman who answered.

"We don't get many calls like this," she said, laughing. "Usually people call because they didn't pay at all." She told me not to worry; the money would be refunded in time; and she congratulated me on my wedding.

"I have to tell you, everything I touch has roses," I said. I told her the story about Rosaria selling us the ring and my grandmother's name.

The woman started to cry. "That is exactly what I needed to hear right now," she told me.

Two days later, the doorbell rang with a flower delivery. The woman from Lord & Taylor's billing service had sent me roses!

Nearly everyone we told reacted with a similar level of emotion to our story. Most people were visibly moved. Even a hairdresser who colored my hair weeks after the wedding was so touched that she tugged down the neck of her shirt to show me that she, too, was covered in roses—she had a vibrant rose tattoo on her neck and others on her chest and shoulders. These reactions made Mark and me even more compelled to share our tale. It was as if our love was so powerful, and we couldn't keep it to ourselves.

When Mark and I realized that we still needed wedding bands, I hadn't spoken to Rosaria in a while. I called Lord & Taylor and asked for her.

"She's not here," a man told me. "Is there something I can help you with?"

"Is she okay?" I asked, sensing something was wrong.

"Are you a friend?"

I explained my connection to Rosaria, and he broke the sad news. She was out of work with a brain tumor. My heart sank.

"I'm so, so sorry," I said.

"Thank you," said the man. "Were you calling because you needed her help with something?"

I explained that Mark and I still needed wedding bands, and I'd been hoping Rosaria could help us.

"You know, it's strange," the man said, "we don't usually sell wedding bands, but there is one here . . . and I think it's yours."

The man said he would credit the sale to Rosaria. When I picked up the ring, it fit perfectly. We found Mark's band at a little jewelry store called Enrico's, and it was just what I'd been hoping for: a ropelike band with a nautical feel. It seemed as though every time I thought about what I needed, I had it within minutes.

It was the same with finding a florist. When Valerie showed us the room with the wedding cake, I mentioned that I loved the flowers and would like to use the same florist if possible. The flower shop, called Forget-Me-Not, was an hour away in North Haven and not a vendor the inn worked with frequently. But, once again, I had a feeling. So, I called the shop and spoke with a woman named Heather.

"Actually, we are available," she said as she looked at the schedule. She sounded surprised. "What are some of your favorite flowers?" she asked. "The Geraldine rose is mine."

"How did you know my name?" I asked her. I hadn't

mentioned it yet.

But she didn't know my name, she explained—the Geraldine rose was a type of rose. She suggested I google it while we were on the phone, and I did.

"You have got to be kidding me," I said when the images showed up on my screen. Geraldine roses were the roses my grandmother had planted around her statue of the Blessed Mother, the ones we always called tea roses.

When I told my mother later that day, marveling over yet another connection to my grandmother, she was skeptical.

"Remember, Ma?" I asked her, excited. "They were all over. I used to cut them and bring them to my teachers."

"Geraldine, you're getting a little too crazy now," my mother said.

I just laughed. I was about to marry the love of my life, and nothing could bring me down.

* * *

Driving back to the Saybrook Point Inn, where I'd spend the last night of my singlehood, I stopped for a traffic light and turned the fan to high. Another hot flash was testing my car's air-conditioning. I glanced in the rearview mirror then, and there in the car behind me was a nun dressed in full habit. The sight itself was unusual, and seeing her coif, wimple, and veil on that hot, muggy, August afternoon, I immediately realized that I had nothing to complain about. I thought of

Sister Eileen and felt so grateful that she had met Mark. *Thank you*, I whispered to her in my thoughts.

The next morning, the day of our wedding, Mark got a similar gift, but we didn't discuss the coincidence until after we were married.

Mark had picked up the *Just Married* banner for the boat—which he had rechristened the *Geraldina* from *Passing Thru*—and he stopped at the church for 9:00 a.m. mass. As he was walking across the parking lot, another car pulled up, and out stepped a nun in full habit. Like me, Mark was a bit surprised. He had never seen her there before.

Mark fell into step with her, and as they entered Saint Mary's, she commented on how beautiful it was. Mark told her, "I'm getting married here today."

After mass, he was starting his car when the nun approached and tapped on his window. "This is my last day as a nun," she said, "and I want to bless your marriage."

Chapter Nineteen

Man and Wife

Two days before the wedding, I drove the car out to Montauk, where Mark and I would be taking the boat after the wedding. It was my last long drive as a single woman, and Mark came to pick me up. Thursday night, our extended families arrived at Rocky's Aqua in Clinton next to Cedar Island Marina for the rehearsal dinner. It was a union of my family and Mark's, as well as a family reunion of my father's and mother's sides of the family, and my brothers and their kids. The dinner was beautiful, and that night I slept alone in the lighthouse, looking out over the vast ocean that had brought Mark and me together. It was in that serene and enchanted setting that I said good-bye to my old life—not with contempt or regret or sadness, but with total peace and acceptance. Because all the roads I'd traveled had led me to this point, I wouldn't have changed a single step. There was just one problem: I couldn't sleep.

The morning of our wedding, the sky was bright, but I was afraid that I looked exhausted. So, I did what I always do when emotion runs high: I turned on the dance music. The night before, Stephanie and her sister, Andrea, had knocked on the door and surprised me with a little silk robe emblazoned with the word *bride*. In the morning, I slipped it on, and I *danced*. Soon, my cheeks were pink, and my eyes shone with the joy that filled me.

I offered up yet another prayer of thanksgiving and asked my grandmother to be with me. And then it was time to get ready.

First, I had a session with a makeup artist from the spa at the inn: just a little bit of eyeliner on top and some extra lashes, some base and a bit of color on my lips and cheeks, but that was it. I'd been trying not to spend too much time in the sun, but my skin still glowed golden brown against my dress.

When the photographer arrived, I was getting my hair done in the lighthouse room. His name was Patrick Colquhoun, and he'd been another providential find—recommended to us by a friend of Mark's. Patrick was a kind and generous person with two adopted children and an amazing eye. My instructions to him had been simple: capture the love.

Unfortunately, at the moment he showed up, I didn't want him to capture anything. The air conditioner in my room had died, and I was sweating like crazy—especially since the hot flashes were starting again. We had to get the mechanic from the inn to come and fix the A/C so my hair wouldn't be ruined. My cousin Stephanie couldn't stop laughing at me and my hot flashes. When it came time to button up my dress, we realized that nobody had the crochet hook typically used to slip satin-covered buttons through their loops, so it took forever to get dressed. Stephanie forgot her special matron-of-honor flip-flops. I forgot the candles for the altar, but Valerie found some for us. It felt like time was speeding up faster than we could keep up with it, but none of the little hiccups could mess with my mood.

As Stephanie piled all our bags into the limo, I was still having intense hot flashes. My poor father started breathing heavily, he was so anxious about being late. But I was still calm.

"Hey guys, they can't have the wedding without the bride, remember?" I said.

If there were a moment I was going to freak out, though, it would have been when the limo overheated and broke down on the way to the church. Even my limo was having hot flashes! We were already ten minutes late, and with a full mass scheduled, we couldn't afford to be any later.

Valerie came to the rescue and sent the inn's shuttle. Arriving at my wedding in a hotel shuttle wasn't exactly what I had in mind, but I couldn't have cared less.

"Wow, you're not even upset," commented the shuttle driver.

I was still in that state of grace, and all I could do was laugh.

Meanwhile, Father Mike *was* getting anxious. He said later that he could picture me running down the road with my shoes in my hand. Margo, a woman from the parish, happened to be driving by and noticed that the doors to the church were still open. She thought that was odd; the ceremony should be underway by now. So, she stopped and went in.

Margo calmed Father Mike down, and then came

out to greet us when the shuttle pulled up. She organized us into a procession, and we finally walked through the big doors of Saint Mary.

Both my mother and father walked me down the aisle. It wasn't just a moment I'd been waiting and wishing for my entire life, it was a moment that was in the hearts of everybody at that wedding.

Mark and I chose to face the altar throughout the ceremony, except for our vows, when we faced each other. So, when Father Mike gave his homily, we were looking right at him. He dedicated his sermon to the rose. He talked about how much he loved the flower as a symbol of God and how the thorns on a rose are meant to protect the precious flower from harm. When the homily was over and Father Mike turned his back, I leaned over to Mark.

"Did you tell him the Rosaria story?" I whispered.

But he hadn't. No one had. After the mass, we found out that Father Mike had a German shepherd named Rosie.

I just looked down at my bouquet of Geraldine roses and smiled. Nothing surprised me anymore.

* * *

Prewedding bloopers aside, everything else went as smoothly as silk. The flowers—white lilies, hydrangeas, and, of course, Geraldine roses—were breathtaking. Nobody could stop talking about the food, not even the globetrotting foodies, Paige and Stan. The truffle pasta was a crowd favorite, as was the raw bar, where Mark's dad, Joe, and my father, looking more handsome than ever, hung out for most of the night.

When our singer and emcee, Marty Q, introduced us for the first time ever as Mr. and Mrs. Mark Giomblanco, our family and friends erupted in thunderous applause. We walked into the room arm in arm, and the atmosphere was absolutely electric. I looked around at my brothers and cousins and aunts and uncles and saw in their eyes the joy that I felt. They had met my boyfriends over the years and consoled me after breakups, and it was as though I could see those scenes flipping through their minds and culminating in this spectacular day. They, too, had been waiting for this moment for thirty years, and they'd come from as far as Florida, North Carolina, Arizona, and Maine to celebrate.

Stephanie's mom, Rita, who always had a hug and words of support for me, had passed away, but there was no sadness that day because I knew she was present, as was my dear uncle Al, with whom I'd washed dishes after many a Thanksgiving dinner at Grandma Brown's house. Uncle Al died the day before the wedding, but he'd sent a beautiful note saying that although he was too old to move around, he'd be with us in spirit. And he was. I saw him in the faces of his daughter, Diane, and her husband, Peter, who came to the wedding anyway, knowing that that's what he would have wanted.

Mark and I danced for the first time as husband and wife to Chris Gaines (the alter ego of Garth Brooks) singing "Lost in You," and then my father, struggling to breathe, summoned the energy to take me in his arms. With tear-filled eyes and a broad smile, he spun me around the dance floor as Louis Armstrong sang "What a Wonderful World."

The love in that room was palpable. I wanted to capture in my heart each magical second: the nieces and nephews and kids of all ages crowding onto the dance floor, *no one* too shy to dance. The middle-aged couples holding hands as if they'd just fallen in love again. Mark's mother, Pat, laughing and smiling and never letting on until after our honeymoon that she'd been diagnosed with cancer. My dad videotaping us when we cut the wedding cake by the water—to the strains of DNCE's "Cake by the Ocean"—and fed bites to each other as the sun went down. For weeks, people told us how they left at the end of the night feeling like they were floating on air.

At the end of the evening, Mark and I returned to the lighthouse room. A bottle of champagne was on ice next to the red roses Mark had sent me for my last night of singlehood with a card that read, "We fit together like hand in glove." We took our glasses out to the balcony and let the moonlight wash over us.

Just below the balcony, a boat had pulled up to the inn's fuel dock, and anglers had hauled a fish the size of a dining room table out of the water. Now, they were starting to butcher it. Mark and I just looked at each other and laughed at the contrast—us in our wedding finery and the fishermen bent to their workaday task—and we offered a toast of gratitude for life in all of its messiness, for the beauty of the stars, for our families and friends, and for our future together. We felt unbelievably blessed.

The next morning, I couldn't resist one more dance. Thinking Mark was still sleeping, I picked up my wedding gown and waltzed it around the room. But Mark caught me, and his smile said that Joe George was right again: I had not let go of that little girl inside me. And we both know that I never will.

We packed up our wedding gifts and took them to the boat, but we didn't unwrap them for a couple of days. We were exhausted, and I wanted us to be completely in the moment when we opened them. Ultimately, we were blown away by the generosity of our guests, many of whom had spent hundreds of dollars just to travel to our wedding. As I knew they would be, the first few hours that Mark and I spent as Mr. and Mrs. Giomblanco were like something out of a fairy tale. And that was only the beginning.

* * *

Honeymooning in Montauk brought another level of meaning to our story. It was where we began, and it was where we chose to start the next chapter. And still, the signs kept coming. Out to dinner one night at Salivar's, we met a woman named Melissa. In a room with a huge shark's head hanging on the wall, we told her the story about Rosaria.

"I have goosebumps," said Melissa, her eyes wide. "Would you believe my aunt's name is Geraldine and my sister's name is Rose?"

"I'd believe anything," I said.

Melissa told us that she had breast cancer, and she invited us to come and say the rosary at Saint Thérèse at a prayer session the church was hosting for her and a pancreatic cancer patient the next day.

"We'll absolutely try to make it," Mark said.

The next day was rainy, but the showers stopped just as we arrived at Saint Thérèse, and a double rainbow appeared over the church. As we opened the door, Melissa called out, "Oh my God, the newlyweds are here!"

A basket of beads was passed around as we prayed the rosary in unison. At the end of the evening, the beads were collected to be turned into rosaries. I asked God for healing—for all those in need of divine love and comfort. I prayed that everyone could learn to speak with the divine.

Walking out of the church, Mark and I passed a framed portrait of Saint Thérèse. I'd seen it before, but this was the first time I'd ever noticed the rose petal tucked into the corner of the frame. Suddenly, I remembered the red spot on my grandmother in the old photo with Stephanie.

"Mark," I said. "That spot on my grandmother was a rose petal!"

I got closer to the portrait to give it a more thorough inspection. Another parishioner noticed my curiosity.

"A woman here was dying," she told me, nodding at the rose petal.

"She asked for our prayers, and someone sent her a bouquet of roses. Inside one of the petals was the image of Saint Thérèse."

"Thank you," I said softly. "Thank you for telling me

that story."

But I wasn't just thanking that woman, I was thanking God. I was thanking Saint Thérèse and Mother Teresa. I was thanking all the guides and angels and saints and everything and anything else that had helped bring me to Mark. And I was thanking my grandma Rosaria.

What my grandmother was always trying to teach me was that God is love, and love is the only reason why we're on this planet. I remembered, again, seeing her sweet, expectant face through that diamond-shaped window in her front door. I remembered how my heart would swell with the purest love when I was in my grandmother's arms again, surrounded by roses. Grandma would be so happy to see me. She would say, "I looooove you," stretching the word out to show how big that feeling was, and she would make that happy little noise as she hugged me: deet, deet, deet. And then I remembered when my grandmother was in a coma years later, when I was an adult, and I visited her in the hospital. I hugged her and made that noise in her ear: deet, deet, deet. And my grandmother opened her eyes.

Like what I have with Mark, what I had with my grandmother was true love. And all true love is a gift.

Sometimes I wonder, still, if Mark was my gift from Grandma Rosaria. Or if maybe the gift is simply this story, this series of incredible experiences that brought Mark and me together. I often think about Joe George, the man in the airport, and one of the very few details he revealed about himself the day we talked: that his mother had a gift for accepting gifts with excitement and humility. Perhaps he saw that ability in me, too, and that was his way of saying that I would someday find my true purpose in life. The more people who are moved by our tale, the more I believe this to be true.

There is a beautiful prayer called the Prayer of Saint Francis, which singer/songwriter Sarah McLachlan set to music and recorded. We played it at our wedding in honor of Sister Eileen, who was a Franciscan nun, and my grandmother Rosaria, who, as an older woman, became an associate of the Franciscan order.

Prayer of Saint Francis

Lord make me an instrument of
your peace
Where there is hatred let me sow
love
Where there is injury, pardon
Where there is doubt, faith
Where there is despair, hope
Where there is darkness, light
And where there is sadness, joy
O divine master grant that I may
not so much seek to be consoled as
to console
to be understood as to understand
To be loved as to love
For it is in giving that we receive
it is in pardoning that we are par-
doned
And it's in dying that we are born
to eternal life

Amen

I believe now that God intends me to be an instrument of faith and hope. I also believe that gifts are meant to be shared. The core of my Catholic faith is that it is better to give than to receive. And so, I share my tale with you. I want to inspire you to dream, to hope, and to open your eyes to the signs that tell you when you are on the right path. Most of all, I hope you will share my story with others, because even a small stone dropped in the water creates ripples that can change lives.

Epilogue

Mysterious Ways

Finding true love is a happy ending, but not in a fairy tale kind of way. Life will *always* present challenges. Mark and I had just moved to Connecticut and were settling in our new home when I got a phone call telling me I would be facing one of those trials.

I'd recently had a physical exam, during which I queried the doctor about my fifteen-pound weight gain, my sleeplessness, and the torrential sweats that had been plaguing me. I was fifty. Was this just part of menopause? As he listened to my heart with his stethoscope, I broke out in one of those heavy sweats.

"How often does this happen?" he asked.

I looked at the imaginary watch on my wrist and said, "Oh, every twenty minutes or so."

He referred me to an endocrinologist. She ran some tests, and she'd just left a phone message for me: "Geraldine," she said, "you need to find a neurosurgeon right away."

There was a five-and-a-half-millimeter adenoma—a benign tumor—pressing on my pituitary gland. I had Cushing's disease.

A serious illness and cranial surgery were the last

things I expected to deal with as a new wife, and yet . . . once again, my grandmother and her heavenly helpers showed their ceaseless presence and support.

Three days before I received that phone call, I'd been cleaning my apartment in Scarsdale after Mark and I moved to our new home in Connecticut. The fact that I was married still felt surreal, and it was bittersweet to be leaving the nest I had created for myself as a single woman. I was sweeping the bedroom when I saw a coin stuck under the baseboard where my bureau had been. I pried it out, and on it was an image of Saint Thérèse, holding roses. It was inscribed: "I am your sister and your friend. I shall always be watching over you."

My grandpa, Rosaria's husband, always carried a Saint Thérèse medal in his pocket, and I have that medal today. But I had never seen this coin before. I treasure it now as a reminder that God has a plan for me.

When I received my first Holy Communion as a girl, I was given the gift of faith. But I had to grow into that faith. Now, I go to mass daily. I want to see God and feel Him and be one with Him. When the saleswoman Rosaria slid the engagement ring onto my finger that day in Lord & Taylor and it fit perfectly, that was God's way of saying to me, "You go, girl!" Writing this memoir has made my faith stronger because I've discovered that baring the source of my sorrow and owning my choices in life has brought a new kind of grace.

While I was working on this book, I struggled with how much of my journey to reveal to readers. I feared that exposing my secrets would turn a romantic love story into something controversial. I feared I would be risking the approval of people I love dearly. As always when I need to calm myself and think, I went to a body of water, which is where I connect most easily with my Creator.

I rode my bike to Clinton's quaint little town beach, and there, I gave up my thoughts to God. As I leaned my bike against a sign post in the sand, I noticed some litter around a trash can. So, I picked up the garbage with an attitude of gratitude—the petition deep within me turned that small chore into a blessing. Then I noticed what looked like a squashed Styrofoam cup beyond a fence, and though my first thought was, "I've done enough. It's not my job to clean up the entire beach," something nudged me, and I went over to pick it up.

To my surprise, it wasn't a flattened cup; it was an index card. And written on it in pink marker was this:

> *I love you to the moon and back.*
> *You are my love of my life my soul*
> *my heat [sic] Remember what I said*
> *before[.] Pretend your [sic] on a*
> *flying unicorn and stay calm[.] you*
> *~~may~~ will stay safe and be protetid*
> *[sic]. I love you SO much and have*
> *a safe flight.*

The moment I read that, I knew what I had to do: I had to ride the unicorn and stay calm. I had to tell the whole truth. This *is* a romantic love story. But it is also a story of a woman who learned to love herself.

Joe George, the man in the airport, told me not to

lose touch with the little girl inside me. I now know that he meant to hold on to the pure, innocent love of a child. I want to give the same message to you: Love yourself. It's never too late. Don't let choices you've made—or other people's judgment of them—destroy that love.

Dig deep inside yourself to find true north on your compass rose. Have the courage to hope and be open to seeing signs that you are on the right path.

I am an ordinary person, just like you, who has felt extraordinary grace. And you can experience it, too.

Acknowledgments

I offer a wholehearted thank you to the following people:

To Grandma Rosaria and my other grandparents; to Saint Thérèse of Lisieux; Saint Teresa of Calcutta; the Blessed Virgin Mary; the Father; the Son, Jesus Christ; and the Holy Spirit for guidance. Loving signs from heaven continue to guide me in my daily life. Thank you to the church staffs at Saint Mary's of the Visitation, Our Lady of Fatima and Mercy by the Sea Retreat and Conference Center. To Sister Eileen Burns and her little sister Rosemarie and to the sisters and associates of Saint Francis, peace be with you.

To Mom and Dad for their amazing unconditional love, which has carried me from singlehood to married life in my fifties. I love you, always and forever.

To my husband's family and to my brothers, Christopher and Richie, and their beautiful families. To dearest friends, Sean and Lori; Kimby, MarMar, Gerri, DiDi, Josie, Angie and to my loving aunts, uncles, and cousins who've supported and loved me as a single person and as a married person. You have blessed my life in more ways than I can list on this page—you know who you are. And to our guests and the service providers at our wedding, it was the best day ever, thanks to you!

Thank you to Jacqueline Burt Cote, a gifted writer who helped me structure the stories captured in the pages of this book. To my editor, Kimberly Caldwell Steffen, who is beyond a great listener and made me feel safe and supported enough to take chances and express myself. To my talented book designer, Michelle Argyle of Melissa Williams Design. To Carol Dannhauser for stating the hard truth, which I admit I had to learn, that there's a difference between telling a story and writing a story. Her insight and counsel enlightened me and encouraged me to publish this book. To Marilyn Allen for her empowering comment that sent me flying high into an unknown zone. "Come here, brave one," she said, ushering me to the front of the room during a pitch contest. Yep, guess who went first?

Thank you to my mentors, angels in disguise, and spiritual guides Joe George, Stephanie Rossi, Eunice Pecora, Susan Garofalo, Arta Habili, Valerie Timreck, Jackie Eiting, Mary Kiley, Robin Miller, Mark Hanson, David Tillman, Dr. David Kruger, Claire Light Coaching, Dr. Arianna Fucini, Catherine Dolan-Haas, Stephanie Shriver-Engdahl, Vanessa Lewis, Mary Hart, and to my role models at Forest City Ratner Company. Thank you, too, to John Bucksbaum, whose open-door policy inspired me to run with big ideas.

To individuals and couples dealing with a secret sorrow and to the retreat leaders and friends at Rachel's Vineyard, I'm forever grateful for your healing touch and blessed ministry. It was sharing in that sacred space that led to the peace in my heart.

I am grateful for Cedar Island Marina in Clinton, Connecticut, and the nooks and crannies of Montauk, New York, where my love story began. These are places where divine providence dwells.

And to my captain, my patient and loving husband, Mark: Without you, Geraldina & the Compass Rose would not exist. My search for peace is complete. I love you.

About the Author

GERALDINE BROWN GIOMBLANCO is a captivating inspirational speaker as well as an author and a strategic mentor coach. A thirty-year veteran of marketing for high-profile shopping centers, she is now dedicated to helping others find their "true north" paths in life and bring those dreams to fruition. Born and raised in Westchester County, New York, she makes her home with her husband on the Connecticut shoreline.

Geri is available for speaking engagements as well as for book readings and signings. She is currently working on her next book. Learn more at gbgbooks.com.

A Note from the Author

God's presence becomes most vivid when I am at the beach or on the water. Or surrounded by loved ones or music or animals—all the things closest to my heart and soul. I invite you to visit gbgbooks.com to view photos of some of these people and places and listen to music that captures the sentiments I describe in each chapter. It's my way of sharing the understanding— the intimate knowing—that God speaks to us where we meet him. I also invite you to be willing and still and listen. And blessed be your journey!

Questions for
Book-Group Discussions

1. What was the gift that Joe George predicted Geraldine would receive?

2. If you were in Geraldine's shoes, would you have married Paul or Philip? How about Ray?

3. Have you ever done something that you knew was wrong on one level but nevertheless you believed was the right decision for you? If so, what effect did that dissonance have on you? Have you come to peace with it?

4. In what way did suppressed sorrow shape Geraldine's adult life?

5. Have you ever experienced a sign from Heaven or from a deceased loved one? If so, what was it and how did it affect your decisions?

6. Does it take courage to follow your intuition? Do you tend to follow gut feelings or dismiss them?

7. How do self-acceptance and compassion for oneself change one's ability to find love?

8. Do you try to be perfect in order to be loved by others, or do you view imperfections as a gift?

9. When you're lost or confused, to whom do you turn for guidance and comfort?

10. In chapter 12, finding Emma Jean in a garbage can and spotting "Fully Rely on God" on a stranger's T-shirt reminded Geraldine of the importance of humility and of the source of her strength. What lessons have you learned in unusual places?